Praise for
*How to Make Money
with Social Media*

"Return on investment in social media is like the weather: Everybody talks about it, but nobody is doing anything about it. With this book, Jamie Turner and Reshma Shah set you up for success with some key fundamentals, and then give you some very specific and illustrative examples on how to calculate the ROI of your social media efforts."

—**Scott Monty,** Global Digital Communications,
Ford Motor Company

"Social media isn't a fad. It's not going away. This book adds tools to your thinking on the matter."

—**Chris Brogan,** *New York Times* bestselling coauthor,
Trust Agents, and publisher, chrisbrogan.com

"Jamie and Reshma have the communication and marketing chops to help anyone leverage social media. Their book reads like a dialogue, not a lecture—just like good social media should. If you've been looking for smart, insightful marketing advice in this space, look no further. You've found it."

—**Andy Goldsmith,** Vice President, Creative & Brand Strategy,
American Cancer Society

"Turner and Shah have crafted a pragmatic guide for marketers, big and small, to use social media to grow a business. Readers will find practical examples and illustrations in detail or easily scanned through the text. Most importantly, the authors address accountability: As marketers must show return on marketing investment, Turner and Shah create a detailed framework to effectively implement and measure social media to generate value for a firm."

—**Chad Mitchell,** IBM Global Business Services and former Principal Analyst, Forrester Research

"Reshma Shah and Jamie Turner have written a practical, down-to-earth guide on how to make money on social media, with the emphasis on practical and down-to-earth. I welcome and recommend it."

—**Al Ries,** marketing consultant and coauthor, *War in the Boardroom*

"There are a lot of reasons I like this book, but I'll give you just two now: First, I like its no-nonsense approach to connect social media and your business goals. And second, it doesn't toss around too many ridiculous acronyms, jargon, or business-speak (which is a pet peeve of mine). Instead, it's written in an accessible voice and engaging style."

—**Ann Handley,** Chief Content Officer, MarketingProfs, and coauthor, *Content Rules: How to Create Killer Blogs, Podcasts, Videos, Ebooks, Webinars (and More) That Engage Customers and Ignite Your Business*

"Social media is a means to an end. Turner and Shah do a brilliant job of concisely getting us to that end. Read this book and you will profit from social media."

—**Erik Qualman,** author, #1 international bestseller, *Socialnomics*

"*How to Make Money with Social Media* is a very practical, user-friendly book on how to use social media for brand building. It is comprehensive, yet conversational, and a joy to read!"

—**Jag Sheth,** Professor of Marketing, Emory University

"*How to Make Money with Social Media* addresses one of the most important issues facing today's businesses. It is an extremely well written guide for managers who need to know how to understand, use, and measure the impact of a medium that is changing the media environment forever."

—**Mickey Belch,** Professor of Marketing, San Diego State University

"This is a must-read for marketing professionals hungry for practical approaches to use social media to build their businesses. Turner and Shah dispense with the hype and focus on what matters most."

—**Ted Woerhle,** CMO, Newell Rubbermaid

HOW TO MAKE MONEY WITH SOCIAL MEDIA

AN INSIDER'S GUIDE ON USING NEW AND EMERGING MEDIA TO GROW YOUR BUSINESS

JAMIE TURNER
AND
RESHMA SHAH, PH.D.

First Printing September 2010

ISBN-10: 0-13-210056-8
ISBN-13: 978-0-13-210056-4

Pearson Education LTD.
Pearson Education Australia PTY, Limited.
Pearson Education Singapore, Pte. Ltd.
Pearson Education North Asia, Ltd.
Pearson Education Canada, Ltd.
Pearson Educación de Mexico, S.A. de C.V.
Pearson Education—Japan
Pearson Education Malaysia, Pte. Ltd.

Library of Congress Cataloging-in-Publication Data:

Turner, Jamie, 1961–
  How to make money with social media: an insider's guide on using new and emerging media to grow your business / Jamie Turner, Reshma Shah.
    p. cm.
  ISBN-13: 978-0-13-210056-4 (hardback : alk. paper)
  ISBN-10: 0-13-210056-8
  1. Internet marketing. 2. Social media—Economic aspects. 3. Online social networks—Economic aspects. I. Shah, Reshma, 1964–II. Title.
  HF5415.1265.T867 2011
  658.8'72--dc22
                        2010026251

Vice President, Publisher
Tim Moore

Associate Publisher and Director of Marketing
Amy Neidlinger

Acquisitions Editor
Megan Colvin

Development Editor
Russ Hall

Operations Manager
Gina Kanouse

Senior Marketing Manager
Julie Phifer

Publicity Manager
Laura Czaja

Assistant Marketing Manager
Megan Colvin

Cover Designer
Chuti Prasertsith

Managing Editor
Kristy Hart

Project Editor
Anne Goebel

Copy Editor
Krista Hansing Editorial Services, Inc.

Proofreader
Kathy Ruiz

Indexer
Joy Dean Lee

Compositor
Nonie Ratcliff

Manufacturing Buyer
Dan Uhrig

To my wife, Dayna, who means the world to me.
And to my children, McKensie, Grace, and Lily,
who, for years, have put up with all my
"wise" sayings.

—Jamie Turner

To my wonderfully supportive husband, Hitesh
Shah, and my darling daughters, Maya and Anya.
Thank you for the time away.

—Reshma Shah

CONTENTS

ACKNOWLEDGMENTS

Okay, this is strange. Here you are, holding this book in your hands, and you've decided to read the Acknowledgments section instead of reading the scintillating content in each and every page of this amazing masterpiece.

Huh?

That means you're either standing in a bookstore waiting for a friend to finish their business in the restroom, or you're hoping we remembered to include your name somewhere in the upcoming paragraphs.

Well, this may come as a surprise to you, but what you're reading is actually the most important section of the book. We're not kidding. After all, writing a book is an amazingly collaborative process. Even though we're the ones who get our names on the cover, this book was written, rewritten, rewritten (again!), and then rewritten one more time all with the help of a wide variety of people. And that was before it even got to the editors, which either means we're terrible writers (entirely possible, by the way) or that we had amazing amounts of great advice and help from our friends, family, and business associates.

With that in mind, we'd like to honor all those who were responsible for this book. Each and every one of you has helped in ways we can never repay. (And, oh, by the way, we're serious when we say we can never repay you. You aren't getting a dime. And Mom, that includes you.)

We'd like to thank the following people: Jennifer Simon, Kyle Wegner, Ann Pruitt, Brent Kuhn, Maribett Varner, Virginia Doty, Rick Skaggs, Kelley Haas, Mike Turner, Jr., Nanci Steveson, Jason Turner, JoAnn Sciarrino-Goggel, Rupal Mamtani, Guy Powell, Karri Hobson-Pape, the volunteers at ASchoolBellRings.org and Kids4Kids360.org, Team Manheim GMSC 2010 Students, and the Beatles (for singing primarily about love and peace).

We'd also like to thank our parents, Dr. Jagdish and Madhu Sheth, as well as Mike and Liz Turner.

Finally, we'd like to thank our friends at Pearson Publishing who have been inspirational throughout. They include Megan Colvin, Anne Goebel, Tim Moore, Amy Neidlinger, Russ Hall, Gina Kanouse, Julie Phifer, Laura Czaja, Chuti Prasertsith, Kristy Hart, Krista Hansing, Kathy Ruiz, Joy Dean Lee, Nonie Ratcliff, and Dan Uhrig.

Thank you all so much. Seriously, this wouldn't have happened without you.

ABOUT THE AUTHORS

Jamie Turner is the Chief Content Officer at the 60 Second Marketer, the online magazine for BKV Digital and Direct Response. He is a leading authority on branding, marketing strategy, and social media who has helped companies such as AT&T, CNN, Motorola, Cartoon Network, and The Coca-Cola Company grow their sales and revenue with outside-the-box marketing techniques. He has been profiled in the world's best-selling marketing textbook and consults with well-known brands around the globe. He is a regular guest on TV and radio programs that focus on marketing and social media, and he is an in-demand keynote speaker for global corporations, events, and trade shows.

Reshma Shah, Ph.D. is an assistant professor in the area of marketing at Goizueta Business School of Emory University. She is also a founder and partner at Inflexion Point Marketing Group. Dr. Shah's marketing insights and strategies have helped companies such as Ciba Vision, GE, IBM, Turner, The Coca-Cola Company, and UPS, among many others, improve their marketing return on investment. Her articles have appeared in several academic journals in the areas of marketing alliances and brand extensions. Dr. Shah was also the recipient of the Distinguished Educator Award at Emory University.

Mr. Turner and Dr. Shah are also cofounders of ASchoolBellRings.org, a nonprofit that builds schools and educational programs for impoverished children around the globe.

IF YOU'RE LIKE A LOT OF PEOPLE, YOU PROBABLY HAVE SOME QUESTIONS ABOUT SOCIAL MEDIA. YOU MAY BE ASKING WHETHER SOCIAL MEDIA IS OVERHYPED, WHETHER SOMETHING ELSE WILL REPLACE IT, OR WHETHER IT'S JUST A BIG, FAT WASTE OF TIME.

Introduction

But the important questions is, "Can I make money with social media?" After all, what's the point of setting up, launching, and running a social media campaign if it's not going to make money?

Well, we've got some good news. You *can* make money with social media—if you follow the right plan. The problem is that many people think that simply updating a Facebook page or uploading a YouTube video is a social media campaign.

It's not.

A well-run social media campaign is a program that's well thought out, well executed, and well managed. It's set up with a clear set of objectives, strategies, and tactics. Most importantly, it's designed to ultimately accomplish one thing: to make money. Everything else is just a stop along the way.

Maybe you're thinking, "I'm just a small business owner, and all of my time goes into running my business. How can I possibly make the time to learn and use social media?" We can tell you from our own experience that social media doesn't have to be time-consuming, especially if you set it up properly from the start.

Or you might be thinking, "I run a huge division of a large global organization. I just need to hire the right people to do my social media." But you can't *delegate* social media until you *understand* social media. And we're here to help you do exactly that.

You might even be thinking, "I work in a business-to-business company where it's all about requests for proposals (RFPs) and low price. Social media doesn't have a place in our company." We're here to tell you that social media isn't just for business-to-consumer companies. In fact, social media can be an extremely effective sales tool for business-to-business companies, too.

If you picked up this book looking for an encyclopedia of marketing theory, this might not be the book for you. Or if you picked it up looking for a simple introduction to the basics of social media, it might not be the book for you, either. But if you're looking for a book that will give you a practical roadmap designed to help you set up, launch, and run a money-making social media campaign, this could be just what you're looking for.

A FEW TIPS ON USING THIS BOOK

We've divided the book into several segments that explore concepts such as the social media landscape, how to get set up for success, different social media platforms, how to integrate social media into your marketing plan, and how to measure social media. All these sections are designed to give you a practical roadmap to help you get going with a successful social media campaign.

We've also included a variety of callout boxes to highlight key ideas in the book. Sometimes you'll see boxes that read "The Big Idea"; other times you'll see boxes titled "Did You Know?" And still other times you'll see boxes titled "Money-Making Tip."

They're all designed to help frame some of the issues in that section of the book.

You'll also see a number of references to additional content located on the 60 Second Marketer Web site. The 60 Second Marketer is an information station for the marketing community sponsored by BKV Digital and Direct Response. We've included several additional pages on the Web site that expand on topics covered in the book. Interested in learning more about a certain topic? Stop by the links mentioned in the book, such as www.60SecondMarketer.com/SeventhDeadlySin or www.60SecondMarketer.com/SocialPromotions.

Finally, you'll notice that we end each chapter with key concepts and action steps that are designed to recap the chapter and review the specific steps to take based on those concepts. The key concepts and action steps aren't there just for grins—use them!

Okay, we've covered a lot of ground here. You're probably eager to get going.

You ready? We are, too. Just turn the page and we'll get started.

PART I

THE SOCIAL MEDIA LANDSCAPE

IS YOUTUBE A WASTE OF TIME? IS TWITTER JUST A FLASH IN THE PAN? CAN FACEBOOK BE USED TO GROW SALES AND REVENUE? CAN SOCIAL MEDIA BE MEASURED? MORE IMPORTANTLY, CAN YOU GENERATE A POSITIVE RETURN ON YOUR INVESTMENT WITH A SOCIAL MEDIA CAMPAIGN?

CHAPTER 1

WHAT SOCIAL MEDIA ISN'T

If these are some of the questions you've asked yourself, then you've come to the right place. Because this is a book designed to answer your questions about social media. More specifically, it's a book that's designed to help you set up, launch, and run a social media campaign that *makes money.* After all, what's the point of running a social media campaign if it doesn't drive revenue?

Social media is a big, complex subject, but before we take a look at the *new* world of social media, let's take a look at the *old* world of traditional marketing. By looking back before we look forward, we'll have a better sense of where social media is going to take us in the future.

MARKETING HAS CHANGED MORE IN THE PAST 5 YEARS THAN IN THE PREVIOUS 100 COMBINED

It's hard to believe, but more marketing changes have occurred in the past 5 years than in the previous 100 years. For perspective on this, let's look back to the starting point for modern marketing. On Christmas Eve 1906, Reginald Fessenden made the world's first radio broadcast. Fessenden sent out a short radio program from Brant Rock, Massachusetts, that included his rendition of "O Holy Night" and ended with a reading from the Bible. And with little more than that, radio was born. Suddenly, companies such as Sears, Coca-Cola, and Ford had the capability to send their advertising messages to millions of people at once.

More than 20 years later, the first television station launched in Schenectady, New York. That station, owned by General Electric, was able to broadcast images as far away as Los Angeles. By September 1928, the station was making four broadcasts a week, although the general population wouldn't widely adopt television until the 1950s.

Then for the next several decades, nothing happened. Sure, there were a few leaps forward (such as the advent of cable TV), but the media used to connect companies to consumers didn't change in any quantifiable way for the entire twentieth century.

Fast-forward to today, when new media appear online monthly or even weekly. What's driving this rapidly changing environment? Put simply, it's the combination of broadband Internet and the wide adoption of personal computers, smart phones, and content tablets such as the Kindle and the iPad. These technological leaps forward have changed the way consumers both receive information and interact with the brands they love.

With change comes opportunity. But if you don't know how to harness these changes, you won't be able to take advantage of the opportunity.

Do you want to learn how to make money with social media? Would you like to find out how to measure the return on investment (ROI) of a social media campaign? Or would you like to see a road map to help you integrate a social media campaign into your existing marketing plan?

To do these things, we start by giving you a deeper understanding of what social media *is*. And the best way to understand social media is to start by talking about what social media *is not*. After all, social media is defined in many ways, so let's zig while other people are zagging and talk about what social media *isn't*.

Did You Know?

Even though the first television broadcast took place in 1928, TV wasn't widely adopted until the mid-1950s.[1]

WHAT SOCIAL MEDIA ISN'T

Some people will tell you that social media is a "here today, gone tomorrow" fad, but those are the same people who are waiting for the eight-track tape deck to come back.

No, social media isn't a flash in the pan. In fact, it'll just keep evolving into something better, which is exactly what happened when personal computers (PCs) first came on the scene.

When PCs first arrived, word processing was about the only thing they were really good for. But then someone figured out a way to connect a few of them. When people started connecting them into expanded networks, they began to understand the true power of the technology.

One of the first services to try to leverage large-scale computer networks was CompuServe, which experienced relatively stable growth during the 1980s and 1990s. CompuServe plugged along fine until America Online (AOL) came along. AOL was the first company of its kind to leverage the power of a user-friendly interface. Thanks to that strategy, AOL grew from 10 million subscribers in 1996 to 27 million subscribers by 2002.

But things didn't last for AOL. When people realized that it was merely an add-on to the Internet, they decided to plug in directly. When *that* happened, the power of interconnected PCs really began to take off. First came early brochure-ware sites; then came blogs; then forums; then bookmarking, tagging, photo sharing, podcasting, virtual worlds, widgets, and ... well, you get the point. Things started to *change*. And they changed in ways that we couldn't even imagine when the personal computer first came around.

That brings us back to our point: The evolution of the personal computer from a simple word processor to a complex web of interconnected minicomputers is similar to the evolution of social media from simple networks to the Web 3.0 technology it's becoming today. Both technologies continue to morph and evolve. And both technologies are here to stay.

With all that in mind, let's keep talking about what social media is *not*.

Social Media Isn't Traditional Marketing

As we've mentioned, traditional marketing is about having a monologue with your customers and prospects. Social media, on the other hand, is about having a *dialogue*. When you have a dialogue with a customer or prospect, the communication is much more fulfilling (and much more profitable).

In the old days, marketing was handled out of a single location (usually called *headquarters*) where a central authority analyzed customer research, sales trends, and demographic information to arrive at a unique selling proposition (USP).

Rosser Reeves of Ted Bates & Company invented the unique selling proposition. The idea was that, by identifying a single, unique point of differentiation for your brand, you could separate your brand from the competition. Reeves used this technique to create a campaign for Anacin that tripled its sales and, during one seven-year run, generated more revenue for Anacin than *Gone with the Wind* had generated in a quarter of a century.

The Big Idea

Traditional marketers focused their energies on what people *thought* about their brands. Contemporary marketers focus their energies on how people *engage* with their brands—online, in stores, at home, and through other channels.

For most of the twentieth century, traditional marketing was pretty simple: Figure out your USP, get the creative people at your agency to come up with a good TV commercial, and run the heck out of it during prime time.

Given how simple marketing was back then, it's no wonder the guys on Madison Avenue had time for three-martini lunches. They didn't have much else to *do*.

But social media is more complex and more fluid than traditional marketing. And it requires an entirely new mindset.

That brings us to our next point ….

Social Media Isn't Just for Young People

A recent study indicated that the fastest-growing segment on Facebook is women older than age 55 and that the largest demographic on Twitter is the 35–49 age group. So, no, social media isn't just for young people. It's for anybody who is interested in using new technologies to grow their sales and revenue.

However, people older than age 35 do take longer to adopt a new technology. Part of the reason is that most humans don't like change, but another reason is that the neural patterns in their brains are already structured for traditional technologies. New technologies require rewiring the brain.

So let's keep going. What else is social media *not?*

Social Media Isn't a YouTube Video

We can't tell you how many times we've heard someone say, "Sure, our company does social media. Just last month, we uploaded our CEO's annual speech onto YouTube."

For starters, let's get something straight: The only person who watched the CEO's annual speech on YouTube was the CEO and, perhaps, his or her family members. Nobody else tuned in. We're serious. Sorry to break the news to you.

Second, just because someone uploaded a YouTube video doesn't mean it's a social media campaign. Social media is about communicating across a wide variety of channels for a sustained period of time. It's not about tossing up a Facebook Fan Page or completing a LinkedIn Company Profile. It's much more than that.

A social media campaign is similar to a marriage. You can't expect to have a good marriage if your primary means of communication is a single conversation for ten minutes every morning. (Trust us, that doesn't work—we know some people who have tried.)

What *does* work is a prolonged, sustained, *two-way* conversation across multiple channels that enables both parties to feel as though they've contributed and they've been heard. When you can accomplish that, your social media campaign is in very good shape.

Did You Know?

A recent University of Massachusetts study indicates that 22 percent of the Fortune 500 have a blog.[2]

Social Media Isn't Always Online

For many of our readers, social media implies some form of *digital* social media or communications enabled through *online* technology. However, we can't forget that a great deal of social media marketing happens offline—after people have turned off their computers.

In a recent study from the Keller Fay Group and OMD, offline communications are still the predominant mode of marketing across a variety of age groups. This study indicated that word-of-mouth is considered to be "highly credible" more often than online conversations.

Despite these trends, we believe numerous experts exist in the area of offline word-of-mouth and that a number of strong books in this area have been written. Therefore, for the purposes of this book, we focus on digital tools and techniques reflecting the booming growth of *online* social media demand.

Social Media Isn't Something That Can't Be Measured

Okay, we're giving our editors heart palpitations because we used a double negative in this heading. But that doesn't mean it isn't true. Social media *can* be measured—and, depending on whom you ask, you can measure it in a dozen or even a hundred different ways. (Hey, look! We said *whom* instead of *who*.)

The great news about social media is that, when you take the time to measure it, you might discover that it is a significant source of profits. Significant profits can make you rich. And we can all agree that money is the only important thing in life.

Okay, that was a joke. Money isn't the only important thing in life. But you get our point—if you measure social media, you can track your ROI. If you track your ROI, you can increase profits. And that's certainly not a bad thing.

We could go on and on about what social media *isn't,* but then the title of the book would be *What Social Media Isn't,* which doesn't strike us as very appealing. So let's keep the ball moving forward and dive into the topic at hand, which is how to make money with social media.

ENDNOTES

1. See http://en.wikipedia.org/wiki/History_of_television.

2. See http://centerformarketingresearch.wordpress.com/2010/ 05/18/social-media-continues-to-be-used-with-higher-education-recruitment/.

THE OWNERS OF THE NEW RED'S PORCH,[1] LOCATED IN A REFURBISHED FIRE STATION IN A TRENDY PART OF TOWN, HAD A BRILLIANT IDEA. THEY WOULD USE THE VIRAL POWER OF SOCIAL MEDIA TO GROW VISIBILITY AND AWARENESS OF THEIR NEW RESTAURANT.

CHAPTER 2

THE EVOLUTION OF MARKETING

Their idea was simple, elegant, and oh-so-viral. They would send tweets that they'd provide a free drink extravaganza at their restaurant if they could get just 100 Twitter followers by the following Monday.

Free drinks. Open bar. No charge.

IN THE WORLD OF MARKETING, THERE ARE TWO SURE-FIRE PROMOTIONS

The first sure-fire promotion is to give away free money. The second is to give away free alcohol, which is exactly what the members of Red's Porch intended to do.

The promotion was so bold and so viral that the biggest concern was not whether it would work, but whether it would overheat the fledgling restaurant. After all, the mainstream media had written stories outlining the success of social media programs such as the one Red's was about to conduct.

Perhaps the best known of these success stories is the one about Dell Computer. Dell had designed a Twitter page called DellOutlet to provide special offers exclusively to people who followed the company. The Twitter page was so successful that it garnered more than 1.5 million followers and generated more than $2.0 million in incremental revenue for Dell.

A typical tweet on the DellOutlet page might read like this:

> *15% off any Dell Outlet business laptop 11z, 15-1545 or*
> *17-1750 laptop with coupon! Enter code at checkout:*
> *PZMKKWHQG7DMM.*

If you were an IT professional (or anybody interested in buying a computer), Dell's offer (available only to DellOutlet Twitter followers) was too good to miss.

Given Dell's success, it wasn't surprising that the owners worried that giving away free alcohol would overheat Red's Porch. The fastest way to kill a good restaurant and bar is to drive too many people to a location, which leads to an overworked wait staff and customers who are frustrated by long lines and a backed-up kitchen.

The owners were a little anxious when they sent their first tweet:

> *Help us grow our Twitter list. If we get 100 followers by*
> *Monday, we will invite all to a free drinks party. OPEN*
> *BAR!!!*

They followed their initial tweet with several more tweets, all promoting one of the most bullet-proof promotions in the history of marketing—free alcohol. During the promotion, the owners checked in periodically to find out how many new followers they had generated.

Did they generate 1,000 new followers? 5,000 new followers? Perhaps 10,000?

Nope. They generated 23 new followers.

What happened? For starters, they didn't have something that we call **social media magnetism.**

With social media magnetism, your brand is so powerful that people are attracted to it the way metal is attracted to a magnet. Your brand is so powerful that people go out of their way to be affiliated and associated with your company because it gives them a sense of style, cache, and panache.

Brands such as Nike, Apple, and Harley-Davidson have tons of social media magnetism, which is why you see people wearing Nike sweatshirts or putting Apple logos on the rear windows of their cars. (Think about it: When was the last time you saw a sweatshirt with a Joe's Plumbing or Nanci's Florist logo on it?)

How to Tell If Your Brand Is a Social Media Magnet

1. Does the general public wear your logo on their sweatshirts?

   __ Yes __ No

2. Does the general public put bumper stickers with your logo on their cars?

   __ Yes __ No

3. Does the general public wear hats with your logo on them?

   __ Yes __ No

If you answered "no" to more than one of these questions, your brand does *not* have social media magnetism. Welcome to the club.

The good news about social media magnetism is that, if you
have it, you can grow your social media program organically.
People actually *want* to be affiliated with brands that have
social media magnetism. They want to have your logo on their
car. They want to wear a sweatshirt with your logo on it. And
they want to be a fan on your Facebook page.

To be a social media magnet, you usually have to spend millions
of dollars and put in hundreds of thousands of man-hours.
Nike, Apple, and Harley-Davidson didn't just happen. They were
part of a concerted effort to build brands that had social media
magnetism. And building those brands took decades, not days.

The second challenge our friends at Red's Porch had was that
they were under the impression that creating a promotion was
the first step in a social media campaign.

But it's not the first step—it's actually the *second* step. The first
step is to use traditional media or word-of-mouth advertising to
drive awareness and traffic to your Twitter, Facebook, YouTube,
LinkedIn, or MySpace pages.

The Big Idea

Brands with social media magnetism attract people to their
social media campaigns more easily than brands that don't have
social media magnetism.

Sure, if you have social media magnetism, you can easily skip the first step and jump to the second step. But if you're like most of us, you'll have to use a lot of the traditional methods to drive awareness. Those methods might include print, radio, and TV (if you're a large, well-funded brand); or e-mail, public relations, and word-of-mouth (if you're a small, underfunded brand).

All this leads us to one of our key points: You can waste a lot of time and money in social media if you don't know what you're doing.

This is where we come in—it's why we wrote this book. Our goal for this book is to give you a tested road map designed to help you make money with social media. Nobody is doing social media because they want to be *social.* They're doing social media because they want to do any combination of these three things:

1. Acquire new customers

2. Get existing customers to buy again

3. Generate referrals from both new and existing customers

But hang on a second. Before we go much further discussing how to use social media to grow your sales and revenues, let's take a quick look at where marketing has been during the past 150 years and where it's headed today. By doing that, we'll have an even better sense of how to set up, launch, and run an effective social media campaign.

WHERE MARKETING HAS BEEN

The first marketing communications firms (then known as advertising agents) started in the 1860s and 1870s. At that time, companies such as N. W. Ayer and J. Walter Thompson wrote the ads and then charged companies a 15 percent commission for publishing them in newspapers and magazines.

In the 1930s and 1940s, the great advertising agencies such as Leo Burnett and Ogilvy & Mather were born. They did such a magnificent job at selling products to consumers that, by the 1950s and 1960s, corporations were clamoring to get the top agencies on Madison Avenue to work on their accounts. CEOs of the world's largest corporations took CEOs of advertising agencies out to dinner to discuss business, profits, and this mysterious new thing called *marketing*.

The agencies had something that the corporations couldn't get their hands on—*creative people*. These were the (mostly) men portrayed on television as martini-drinking, skirt-chasing prima donnas whose magic touch on an ad could make the difference between a profitable quarter and an unprofitable one.

Ahhhh, if it were still only that simple.

But time marches on. By the 1980s, the power began to shift away from Madison Avenue to the corporations. Corporations seemed to believe that their success revolved not around the creative, but around *strategy*. They thought that the most important part of a marketing campaign wasn't the headline or the visual; it was the *strategy* behind the headline or the visual.

The people who could think up the best strategies came from schools such as Stanford, Harvard, and Wharton. So the corporations started hiring their MBAs, and the power shifted away from Madison Avenue to the corporate side of the equation.

This was all fine and dandy (if you were on the corporate side). Ad agencies that were still populated with smart, hard-working marketing experts had to cede power to the corporations they worked with.

Fast-forward to the 1990s, when data and information became the king and queen of marketing. Suddenly, the center of power wasn't in the advertising agencies. Nor was it in the corporations. It shifted to companies (such as Walmart, Home Depot, and Office Depot), who, with their highly sophisticated logistics and data management programs, were able to slice and dice information to such a degree that they could tweak distribution not only on a city-by-city level, but also on a store-by-store level.

That power shift—from the ad agency, to the corporation, to the retailer—all happened during the last half of the twentieth century. For decades, the advertising gurus on Madison Avenue were in charge of the brand. Then the MBAs took over. And for a while, the retailers were in charge.

But today a quantum shift has occurred in who controls the conversation about the brand. It's no longer solely the agency, the corporation, or the retailer. *It's the consumer.* The consumer is in charge of your brand as much as you are, and what they think and say about it can spread around the globe at the speed of light (see Figure 2.1).

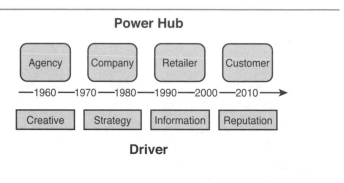

Source: Dr. Reshma Shah, Emory University

Figure 2.1   The power brokers in marketing have evolved during the past 50 years.

In 1965, a brand such as Coca-Cola or Pepsi could communicate with 85 percent of the viewing TV audience by running three prime-time commercials. That's right, any brand that could run just three commercials in prime time could connect with the vast majority of people who were watching TV.

But by the early 2000s, the same brands had to run more than 125 commercials to achieve the same results. Why? Because of the fragmentation of the viewing audience across dozens (or hundreds) of cable channels.

Then with the wide adoption of broadband Internet, platforms such as YouTube, Facebook, LinkedIn, Twitter, and MySpace took center stage. When content distribution shifted to those platforms, the consumer started having as much control over the brand as the agency, the corporation, or the retailer.

SOCIAL MEDIA COMES OF AGE

The consumer has taken control of your brand's position in the marketplace. For evidence of this, just ask United Airlines. More than eight million people watched a YouTube video entitled "United Breaks Guitars," written by a musician named Dave Carroll after the airline allegedly refused to repair his guitar that was broken on a United flight. According to one source, the company's stock price dropped nearly 10 percent the week after the video went viral.

Or ask Motrin, which had to yank a video targeting mothers who carry their babies in slings when complaints about the video started to boil over. Never mind the fact that subsequent research indicated that the average consumer actually *liked* the commercial. By the time things started to heat up online, it was already too late.

Or ask Toyota, which spent decades building one of the more powerful brands in history, only to have it horribly tarnished because of its slow, methodical, and bureaucratic response to the sudden acceleration issues.

The bottom line is this: If you're a brand manager, a chief marketing officer, or anybody who has an interest in the success of your marketing program (which should be 100 percent of the people working at your company), you should be aware that you no longer own your company's brand. The consumer does. And that's both an opportunity and a threat.

The Big Idea

Consumers have as much control over your brand's perception as you do. By nurturing your relationship with them, you can create brand advocates who will do the selling for you.

If you're like some people, you might find this whole social media thing a little scary. In fact, you might even wish you could go back to the good old days of traditional media. But hang tight—we're about to show you some innovative and effective ways to use social media to grow your business.

You have a lot to learn, and things are changing rapidly. But if you follow the road map outlined in this book, you'll soon have a solid social media program that's generating real revenue and profits for you and your company.

So open your mind and take a step back. We're about to show you how to set up, run, and manage a social media program designed to effectively and efficiently grow your sales and revenue.

Before we move on to the next chapter, let's take a look at the key concepts and action steps we've covered in this chapter.

▶ **Key concept:** A social media magnet is a brand that people want to be associated with. Your brand is probably not a social media magnet.

▶ **Action step:** Accept the fact that your brand is not a social media magnet and begin developing marketing campaigns and promotions designed to attract prospects and customers to your social media program.

▶ **Key concept:** Successful social media campaigns are designed to do three things: 1) Acquire new customers, 2) Get existing customers to buy again, and 3) Generate referrals from both new and existing customers.

▶ **Action step:** Don't lose sight of those three goals as you build your social media campaign. Plenty of distractions will arise, but you need to keep those three goals front and center.

▶ **Key concept:** The center of power for your brand is no longer the agency, the corporation, or the retailer. It's the consumer.

▶ **Action step:** Honor the consumer in everything you do. Be transparent. Also give consumers what they need to become advocates for your brand.

ENDNOTES

1. The Red's Porch case study is based on a real restaurant and actual events. We've changed the name to protect the innocent.

GOOGLE LISTS MORE THAN 136 *MILLION* WEB PAGES UNDER THE SEARCH "MAKE MONEY WITH SOCIAL MEDIA." EVEN MORE FASCINATING IS THAT A DISPROPORTIONATE NUMBER OF THE ENTRIES FOR THIS TOPIC AREN'T WORTH A DIME. THEY JUST DON'T OFFER ANYTHING THAT'S REAL, SUSTAINABLE, AND LEGITIMATE.

CHAPTER 3

How to Think About Social Media

But that's why we're here. And it's why you're reading this book—because you're committed to cutting through all the garbage and learning real, legitimate ways to make money with social media.

If you want to use social media to grow your sales and revenue, a great starting point is to reframe how you *think* about social media. By putting social media into context, you'll be able to shape it into what you need for your business. And perhaps the best way to do that is to look back at some of the historical parallels.

Did You Know?

Although radio was first introduced in 1906, it took years for it to catch on. Not so with social media, which has gained wide adoption at a much more rapid pace.[1]

As hard as it might be to believe, when radio was first introduced in the early twentieth century, people were confused by the whole concept. One news headline from the *Daily News* read, "Radio confuses people. Many go back to playing horseshoes instead."

Okay, so the newspaper headline *didn't* say that. But you get our point. People found radio perplexing. Why? Because it was a new paradigm (which is just a fancy way to say that people hadn't seen anything like it).

When people encounter something new (such as radio, TV, or social media), they often feel threatened or scared. People might have said comments such as these about radio when they first came across it in the early twentieth century:

▶ "It has a bunch of scary-looking knobs and buttons."

▶ "It requires electricity, which could kill me."

▶ "When I turn it on, little people inside the box start talking to me."

▶ "Mr. Jones listens to his every night. I've always thought he was a little odd."

▶ "I've seen the entire Smith family huddled around theirs. I've never liked the Smiths, especially their dog."

Now for some good news. Social media isn't anything to be scared of. It can even be your friend. Better still, if you think about social media in the right way, you can use it to grow your business.

GETTING FAMILIAR WITH SOCIAL MEDIA

The first step to making money with social media is to wrap your mind around it. And the easiest way to wrap your mind around social media is to draw comparisons to other things you might be familiar with.

Let's start with social media in general.

What is social media? You can find dozens of answers on the Internet, some helpful and some flat wrong. But for our purposes, social media are the digital tools that enable a two-way conversation between your prospects or customers and your business.

Unfortunately, most businesses use social media for one-way monologues instead of two-way dialogues. This brings us to our first analogy:

Social media is more like a telephone than a megaphone.

The Big Idea

It's easy to wrap your mind around social media when you draw a parallel between social media and something you're already familiar with. For example, using social media is similar to using a telephone to have a two-way dialogue. In contrast, using traditional media is similar to using a megaphone to broadcast a one-way message.

Businesses that use social media as a megaphone are missing the point. You know the kind we're talking about. They're the businesses (or consultants) that can't stop talking about themselves and what makes their products or services special.

But have you ever been on a date with someone who can't stop talking about how wonderful he or she is? Have you ever been out with someone who constantly bragged and never once asked you about your interests?

We're guessing here, but we imagine that if you went on a date with someone like that, it was probably the last date you had with him or her.

So back to our analogy—using social media is similar to using a telephone, not a megaphone. And telephones are meant for dialogues, not monologues.

KEY SOCIAL MEDIA PLATFORMS

Now let's take that analogy a step further. If using social media is similar to using a telephone, then what is Facebook like? Or LinkedIn? Or Twitter?

We developed some analogies.

Did You Know?

Recent data shows that Facebook has more monthly unique visitors (135 million) than MySpace (47 million), Twitter (21 million), and LinkedIn (15 million) combined.[2]

> ▶ **Facebook is like a pub.** It's a casual place where you can go to talk about what you did over the weekend, tell a dirty joke, or tell people about the checkers convention you attended last week. (*Side note:* If you actually *did* attend a checkers convention, we suggest that you replace the phrase "checkers convention" with "mountain climbing convention" before announcing it to your Facebook friends.)

▶ **LinkedIn is like a trade show.** You wouldn't tell people at a trade show what you did in Vegas last weekend, would you? Okay, maybe *you* would, but the average businessperson wouldn't. Limit LinkedIn to your professional side. Talk about business. Talk about interesting articles in the *Harvard Business Review.* And use plenty of phrases such as "value chain" and "business model" in your profile. That should do the trick.

▶ **Twitter is like a cocktail party.** Just be sure you send out tweets that are helpful. New Tweeple make the mistake of taking Twitter seriously when its home page asks, "What are you doing now?" Well, we've got some bad news for you. Nobody cares what you're doing now. They care about information that will help them in their daily lives. So stick with helpful tweets that will position you (or your company) as an expert, drive people to a landing page on your site, or promote someone else in your industry who will someday return the favor.

▶ **YouTube is like Times Square on New Year's Eve.** Times Square on New Year's Eve is packed with people clamoring for attention, which illustrates the problem. Just as it's hard to stand out in Times Square, it's hard to stand out on YouTube. Too much competition exists. So if you want to use YouTube to make money, you need to build awareness for your YouTube channel first. (You do have a YouTube channel, right? No? Then get hopping and go set one up right now. We tell you how to use it in an upcoming chapter.)

Did You Know?

The average YouTube video is only 2 minutes and 46 seconds long. Despite that, it would take you more than four centuries to watch all the videos on YouTube.[3]

▶ **MySpace is like Woodstock.** MySpace has suffered the same fate as AOL—it was huge at one time, but it has faded a little during the past few years. That said, MySpace still provides some very good uses. If you're a musician or a cause-oriented marketer, you should be all over MySpace. But if you're selling industrial widgets in the business-to-business (B2B) space, you should do two things: 1) avoid MySpace like the plague and 2) think about getting a new job, because selling industrial widgets in the B2B space sounds like a terribly boring job.

OTHER SOCIAL MEDIA PLATFORMS YOU SHOULD KNOW ABOUT

One of the more common mistakes people make when thinking about social media is to think that social media is about only Facebook, LinkedIn, Twitter, YouTube, and MySpace. In reality, social media is about much more.

You should also be familiar with these social media tools:

▶ **Blogs**—Digital magazines or diaries that are often written in an informal, chatty style.

▶ **Bookmarks and tags**—Similar to digital yellow stickies that let other members of the online community know that you like an article or a Web page.

▶ **E-mail newsletters**—Digital flyers that let people know about your products or services.

▶ **Widgets**—Online gadgets that help you crunch numbers, check the weather, or find out how much money you made (or lost) in the stock market today.

▶ **Content aggregation sites**—Sites that effectively cut out articles from other online newspapers and repost them in one central location.

▶ **Wikis**—Sites that enable large groups of people to contribute and edit content.

▶ **Voting**—Gives people the opportunity to express their opinion on a product or service.

▶ **Crowdsourcing**—Uses the talents of many people in different parts of the globe to contribute to something (such as the development of an open-source software program).

▶ **Discussion boards and forums**—Places where people can digitally thumbtack their thoughts, comments, or suggestions on a digital cork board hosted on your Web site.

▶ **Backchannel sites**—Places where people at trade shows and conventions can comment on the event or the speaker on stage. (Side note: Always check your zipper before doing a speech where backchannel sites are available. We learned that one the hard way.)

- **Tweetups**—Meetings or casual get-togethers that are organized via Twitter (such as "Meet us as Bob's Tavern at 6:00 pm. We're getting together to discuss the checkers convention … I mean, the mountain climbing convention").

- **Photo-sharing sites**—Digital photo albums on sites such as Flickr, Kodak Gallery, and Snapfish where people can upload their favorite photos.

- **Podcasting**—A way for small and large organizations to broadcast their thoughts, comments, or perspectives on a wide variety of topics.

- **Presentation-sharing sites**—Places where you can upload your latest and greatest PowerPoints. (Why would you do that? To position yourself as a thought leader.)

- **Virtual worlds**—Places where (young) people go to create second lives.

- **Ratings and reviews**—Enable people to rate your product or service and write reviews. (Believe it or not, negative reviews can actually help your brand because they give you instant customer feedback.)

What does all this mean? The bottom line is that the world is changing at a rapid pace, and it will change only faster in the future. You have a choice: Wrap your mind around social media and use it to make money, or get left in the dust when your competition beats you to it.

Which side will you be on?

SOCIAL MEDIA MODELS USED BY THE FORTUNE 500

Whether you work as a sole proprietor or at a Fortune 500 company, it's a good idea to know how others are using social media so you can incorporate those models into your own campaigns.

With that in mind, here are five social media models that are used by the Fortune 500 (some of whom are our own clients):

- ▶ **Branding.** Some companies use social media strictly as a branding tool. Typically, this means running a YouTube campaign that (hopefully) gets a lot of buzz around the water cooler. In our opinion, using social media simply as a branding tool is a twentieth century mindset. If you really want to supercharge your social media campaigns, you'll incorporate one or all of the next four highly measurable approaches.

- ▶ **eCommerce.** If you can sell your product or service online, then you'll want to drive people to a landing page on your website where they can buy your goods. How can you accomplish this? Just do what Dell does—they Tweet about special promotions available only to the people who follow them on Twitter. The promotional links are easily tracked so they can see how many people went to the landing page and how many converted from a prospect to a customer. They generate millions of dollars in revenue each quarter by using this method.

- ▶ **Research.** Many companies are using social media as a tool to do research. Sometimes, this involves building a website to track the results. Starbucks has done this famously with their MyStarbucksIdea.com website. Other times, using social media as a research tool can be as simple as doing a poll on LinkedIn, SurveyMonkey, or via email.

- ▸ **Customer Retention.** A good rule of thumb is that it costs three to five times as much to acquire a new customer than it does to keep an existing one. Given that, wouldn't it be smart to use social media as a tool to keep customers loyal and engaged? That's what Comcast and Southwest Airlines do—they communicate via Twitter, Facebook, and other social media platforms to help solve customer service issues.

- ▸ **Lead Generation.** What do you do if you can't sell your product or service online? Then you'll want to do what many B2B companies do—that is, to use social media to drive prospects to a website where they can download a whitepaper, listen to a Podcast, or watch a video. Once you've captured the prospect's contact information, you can re-market to them via email, direct mail, or any number of other methods.

Let's review several key concepts and action steps from this chapter before we move on:

- ▸ **Key concept:** It's easy to wrap your mind around social media when you draw parallels between it and something you're more familiar with.

▶ **Action step:** Review the different parallels between platforms such as YouTube, Facebook, and Twitter and things you're already familiar with (such as a pub). Share those parallels with people in your office so they can get comfortable with these new tools, too.

▶ **Key concept:** Social media is about more than just YouTube, Facebook, Twitter, and LinkedIn.

▶ **Action step:** Broaden your understanding of the various social media tools by visiting several blogs, forums, e-newsletters, and other platforms you might not have visited.

▶ **Key Concept:** There are five different social media models used by the Fortune 500.

▶ **Action Step:** Use one or more of these models for your own social media campaign. Better still, evolve one of these into a brand new approach that's even better than these originals.

ENDNOTES

1. See http://en.wikipedia.org/wiki/History_of_radio.
2. See http://blog.compete.com/2009/02/09/facebook-myspace-twitter-social-network/.
3. See http://youtube-global.blogspot.com/.

YOU'RE INTERESTED IN LEARNING HOW TO USE SOCIAL MEDIA TO GROW YOUR SALES AND REVENUE. THAT'S GOOD. BUT BEFORE WE DIVE INTO THE SPECIFICS OF MAKING MONEY WITH SOCIAL MEDIA, WE NEED TO TALK ABOUT THE *LANGUAGE* OF SOCIAL MEDIA. AFTER ALL, THE STARTING POINT OF ANY GOOD CONVERSATION IS LANGUAGE, RIGHT?

CHAPTER 4

THE LANGUAGE OF SOCIAL MEDIA

One of the big issues surrounding the language of social media is whether it's singular or plural. The word *media* is plural, but we're not big fans of saying, "Social media *are* the next big thing," when most people are saying, "Social media *is* the next big thing."

We're aware that we're breaking all sorts of rules by doing that, and we're reasonably sure our use of social media in the singular will lead to the downfall of Western civilization. But our goal in the conversation we're having with you is to talk with you in plain, honest language that's as clear and easy-to-understand as possible.

Make sense?

GETTING SOCIAL MEDIA VOCABULARY STRAIGHT

We should discuss a few other terms before we continue, such as the differences in a social medium, a platform, and a channel:

- ▶ **Social medium**—Any single, broad category of tool that you use to run a social media campaign. A blog, a forum, and a user-generated video site are all examples of a social medium.

- ▶ **Platform**—The software or technology you use within a social medium. For example, WordPress is a platform used for blogging, and YouTube is a platform used for online video.

- ▶ **Channel**—The specific, individual connection between you and your customer. Examples of social media channels include your specific blog, Twitter account, and Facebook profile.

We need to explain one thing that might have been on your mind. Many people have described social media as a silver bullet for your business. They've written blog posts, posted YouTube videos, and even written books talking about how social media is "transformative" and "the next big thing." (Yes, we see the irony in this.)

The result is that social media has become overhyped—and we mean *really, really overhyped.*

Social media isn't a cure for everything that ails your business. And it's not a silver bullet that you can turn on to solve all your problems. But it is a viable, long-lasting marketing tool that, when used properly, can help you grow revenues, increase customer loyalty, and build awareness. And that's not such a bad thing, right?

THE SOCIAL MEDIA LIFE CYCLE

Social media isn't the first new technology to be overhyped. Think back a few years ago when Web logs, now known as blogs, gained traction. Corporations, nonprofit groups, and individuals all jumped onto the blogging bandwagon.

The more these entities adopted blogging as a viable communications tool, the more blogs were positioned as a silver bullet that would easily solve just about any marketing problem. For a while, it seemed as though every CEO at a Fortune 500 company had a blog.

But then a funny thing happened. People realized that blogs weren't going to solve all their problems, so they grew disenchanted. Suddenly, people viewed blogs as a waste of time. People decided they didn't have time for blogs, especially blogs that nobody read.

But blogs didn't die. They just evolved into something better and more useful. Instead of using blogs as press release distribution tools, CEOs (and other members of corporations) began using individual blogs as channels to have *conversations* with their prospects and customers. When the conversations happened, people began to recognize how to best use a blog.

Companies now realize that their blogs are channels that can create a link between a customer or prospect and a business. And when they build that link, they're creating loyalty for their brand and their product or service.

With that in mind, it's important to note that social media will move through an overhyped stage and into a stage in which people discount its importance or effectiveness. And as with any roller-coaster ride, it'll be a little scary for a while. But if you manage the expectations of those around you and help them understand the value of social media, the ride won't be quite so bumpy.

Better still, if you follow some of the social media business models we're about to discuss, you might be able to bypass the scary stage and move right into the productivity stage.

BRINGING YOUR SOCIAL MEDIA CAMPAIGN TO LIFE

The model illustrated in Figure 4.1 isn't the only social media business model, but it's the model that companies such as Dell and Papa John's Pizza have used to build their social media programs. Essentially, customer prospects are driven to social media channels that the parent company sponsors or manages. In Dell's case, the company uses Twitter.com/DellOutlet as a way to promote special offers to the more than 1.6 million people who follow them on that Twitter page. When a special offer is posted on the DellOutlet page, it drives customer prospects to a landing page on the company's Web site that has been specifically set up to match the offer on the DellOutlet page. If the offer is appealing enough, a small percentage of Dell prospects will convert to Dell customers. With that data and information now captured in their system, Dell can remarket to those members of the Dell social media community who landed on the Dell site via Twitter.

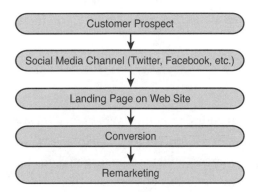

Figure 4.1 You can measure social media on a return on investment (ROI) basis, particularly if you use business models such as this one.

To drive prospects to the social media channel, Dell (or any other corporation) can use different types of traditional and nontraditional media. The company could use direct mail, radio, or outdoor advertising to make people aware of the social media community it's created. Or, more likely, Dell could use blogs, forums, and online video to generate traffic. If a company is really sophisticated, it uses contextual advertising or behavior targeting to drive traffic to its social media site.

A contextual ad is a paid search or banner ad placed near similar content on a blog, forum, or online article. If you own a hunting lodge in Montana and you want to attract customers to your lodge, it would make sense to place a banner ad near an article or blog post that's about rifles, shotguns, hunting, or other outdoor activities, right? By running ads that are contextually sensitive, you increase the click-through rate. And when you increase the click-through rate, you increase your profits.

Ahhh, profits. Nice!

What about behavioral targeting? What's that all about? Behavioral targeting is similar to contextual ads, but with a few important differences. Behaviorally targeted ads follow groups of people around the Internet. For example, tens of thousand of people each day type "cameras" or "camera gear" into Google, Yahoo!, or Bing. A certain percentage of those people click through to Web sites that contain information about cameras that'll help them make decisions about their next camera purchase. But most people don't finalize their decisions about buying a camera in just a few clicks. Typically, they surf the Web on several different occasions, continuing to gather information before they spend $900 on a new camera.

Wouldn't it be cool if, as those thousands of people surfed the Web reading more articles about cameras, they saw an ad for your brand of camera? Wouldn't the click-through rate be higher if ads for your camera gear followed people around the Net as they surfed for more information about cameras?

That's behavioral targeting, and it's a great way to make the shopping and purchase experience even more relevant. Now, before you get all up-in-arms about privacy issues, remember that advertisers aren't following *you* around—they're following *statistical data* around. Nobody is snooping around your computer. They're just serving up ads to Web sites that thousands of people like you happen to be reading on a topic of interest that you share.

Did You Know?

Privacy advocates have raised some questions about behavioral targeting, but behavioral targeting uses the same techniques that the direct mail industry has been using for decades. The direct mail industry uses statistical data about large groups of people to send targeted messages to interested buyers. Behavioral targeting uses the same techniques.

So how does this relate to the social media model we outlined previously? It's an example of how savvy businesses can use sophisticated online tools such as contextual ads and behavioral targeting to drive people to social media sites that ultimately lead to landing pages where they can buy your product.

Some people might ask, "Why wouldn't I use contextual ads or behavioral targeting to drive people *directly* to my landing page? Why would I send them to my social media sites first?"

The short answer is, that's definitely one approach. Driving people directly to your landing page is a quick, easy way to drive traffic to your Web site. But what happens when you start losing efficiencies on that model? What happens when people aren't clicking through on those ads as frequently as they used to?

When that happens, you add the next component, which is to use every form of media that you can (both traditional and nontraditional) to drive people to your social media channels. It's an additional way to add volume to your overall marketing campaign. Better still, it's an additional way to build a relationship with your customers and prospects.

KEEPING CUSTOMERS FOR LIFE

The concept of a relationship is worth pausing and thinking about for a second. Remember when we said that the whole idea behind a social media campaign is to have a two-way conversation with your customers and prospects? When you have a two-way conversation with customers and prospects, you're doing more than just having a conversation. You're building a *relationship,* too. Relationships happen over time, and they often happen *before your customer is ready to buy.*

Why is this so important? Because not all your customers are ready to buy at the same time. One consumer behavior model that highlights this is the Awareness, Interest, Desire, and Action (AIDA) model. This model has been used since the 1960s to highlight the process that consumers go through when they buy a product. If one person is in the awareness stage and another person is in the action stage, they have different buying mindsets. If you do things right, you'll send different pieces of communication to each of those consumers to address where they are on the AIDA decision-making process.

Let's look at a quick illustration of how to use the AIDA model when thinking about your social media campaign. If someone buys a car every five years, wouldn't it be a good idea to begin nurturing your relationship with that consumer sometime in year 4? That way, you can build awareness, interest, and desire during the course of a year, which will ensure that, in year 5, your brand is at the top of the list when the buyer is ready to take action.

Let's recap a few of the key concepts we've covered and talk about action steps for those concepts:

▶ **Key concept**—A social medium is the category of tool a company is using to run a campaign. A platform is the software or technology used within a social medium. And a channel is the specific, individual connection between you and your customer.

▶ **Action step**—Learn these terms so that everyone within your company is using the same language to discuss your social media campaign.

▶ **Key concept**—Many different corporations are using several social media models. The most common model is customer/prospect → social media channel → landing page → conversion → remarketing.

▶ **Action step:** Set up your social media campaign so that it follows this basic model, which enables you to track results, adjust your campaign, and improve your ROI.

▶ **Key concept:** You can use traditional media and nontraditional media to drive traffic to your social media sites. The more traffic you drive to these sites, the more opportunity you have to build a long-term relationship with these prospects.

▶ **Action step:** Nurture your relationship with your prospects by providing them useful tools and information that benefits them. Don't always sell, sell, sell. Sometimes a more nurturing, helpful approach builds a deeper loyalty.

▶ **Key concept:** The Awareness, Interest, Desire, and Action (AIDA) model is a consumer behavior model that highlights where people are in the buying process.

▶ **Action step:** Customize your marketing campaign so that it talks to prospects differently, depending on where they are in the buying cycle.

PART II

HOW TO SET YOURSELF UP FOR SOCIAL MEDIA SUCCESS

THE AVERAGE TENURE
FOR A CHIEF MARKETING
OFFICER AT A MIDSIZE TO
LARGE CORPORATION IS
JUST 11 MONTHS. THAT'S
PRETTY SCARY.

CHAPTER 5

LAYING THE GROUNDWORK FOR
SUCCESS

Part of the problem is that most CMOs have difficulty figuring out how to measure their marketing campaigns. That's understandable—just a few years ago, the formula for marketing success was to develop a 30-second television spot and run the heck out of it. Things have changed since then.

Back in the day, if you had a 30-second spot that made people laugh or cry, you were sitting pretty. And if that emotional connection actually resulted in *sales,* crazy things could happen for you, including promotions and raises.

The truth is, during the twentieth century, marketing was more about the *creative* than it was about the *media.* If you were lucky and had a "Polar Bears" or "Caveman" commercial on your hands, you'd keep pumping more money into the campaign and watching sales rise. You'd keep doing that until sales started to lag. Then you'd start everything all over again.

Figure 5.1 illustrates our point. The *y*-axis represents marketing expenditures, and the *x*-axis represents sales. The slope *(m)* represents the impact marketing has on sales. The steeper the slope, the greater the impact.

So if you had a "Caveman" commercial on your hands (that is, a commercial that had emotional appeal *and* made the cash register ring), you would continue adding to the marketing budget as long as the slope was in positive territory.

Marketing Expenditures

Figure 5.1   The slope (m) represents the impact marketing has on sales.

An example of a slightly more complex formula for all this is $a + bx_1 + cx_2 + dx_3 + ex_4 = y$, where a = traditional media, b = social media, c = price, d = distribution, e = product mix, and y = profits. The variables signified by x_1, x_2, x_3, and x_4 all influence the campaign and will ultimately have an impact on the profits.

MEASURING WHAT COUNTS

We're not trying to freak you out with a bunch of formulas and charts. In fact, that's probably the only true formula you'll read in this book. We're simply trying to highlight the importance of using some pretty simple tools to measure the impact of your social media campaign. The more diligent you are about measuring your social media campaign, the less likely you are to be one of those chief marketing officers who lasts only 11 months.

Consider this interesting statistic: According to a survey by
Mzinga and Babson Executive Education, only 16 percent
of those polled said they currently measured the return on
investment (ROI) for their social media programs (see Figure
5.2). More than four in ten respondents didn't even know
whether the social tools they were using had ROI measurement
capabilities.

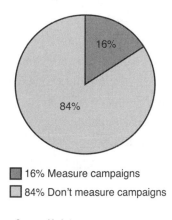

Professionals Worldwide Who
Measure the ROI of Social Media

■ 16% Measure campaigns
□ 84% Don't measure campaigns

Source: eMarketer.com

Figure 5.2   Only 16 percent of marketers around the globe measure their
social media campaigns on an ROI basis.

You don't have to be one of the 84 percent who don't measure
the ROI of their social media campaigns. You can be one of the
16 percent who can track the results—if you follow the plan
outlined in this book.

At a recent conference on social media, Rupal Mamtani, the founder and CEO of upscale furniture store Global Living, said, "I spend almost two to three hours a day personally on the social media marketing efforts for Global Living. I have to be the one involved. I can't outsource my Tweets. No one else has the perspective around this business the way I do. I represent the brand. Having said that, it's exhausting running the business 24/7 and managing to be the face of the brand."

When asked about the impact all her effort has had on her company's performance, she said, "After six months of being somewhat of a pioneer in the social media space in my industry, I am just now beginning to see results. People are beginning to engage more with me and with the company." She has not seen a direct impact on sales yet, but she sees more engagement, which could result in leads. *Leads,* she reiterates—not sales. For this CEO, social media is a supplement to traditional media, at best: "It won't replace newspaper advertising, a billboard, or even an event—at least, not in my business."

Clearly, Mamtani sees value in her social media involvement but still wonders when she'll see a return on the personal time she invests. Of course, the primary purpose of any kind of traditional marketing communication is to inform, persuade, or remind your customers about your product or service in an attempt to gain either a new sale or repeat sales. In the process, the hope is that your customers will become engaged with your organization or brand in a meaningful way that encourages them to keep coming back for more.

The good news for Mamtani is that she ultimately has her sights set on the only thing that really matters: social media's impact on sales. The fact that she's just beginning to see a link between the two is good news and, hopefully, is a sign of better things to come.

RISKS ASSOCIATED WITH SOCIAL MEDIA CAMPAIGNS

One multidivisional communications company we interviewed saw the benefits of engaging in social media but also identified several risks associated with it. The company currently has no formal organizational structure for managing the social media platforms and conversations across areas within the company, between the corporate office and the satellite locations, and between the company's buyers and sellers.

To ensure that conversations through social media marketing are meaningful, the company makes a large investment in people, technology, and process. The company also believes that it will have to invest a great deal in research to understand just how social media impacts sales compared to other forms of marketing. With platforms and tools in social media evolving so rapidly, marketing heads are much more comfortable adopting a "wait and see" approach, to avoid making inefficient and ineffective investments in the social media space. And they're not alone.

Recent conversations with the chief marketing officer of another multibillion-dollar multidivisional company uncovered a similar sentiment. It's clear that this company understands the importance of adopting social media for its brands; however, the main concern is scalability. How can several thousand people connected though some common platform at a given point in time spark millions of consumers to take action?

Corporate Social Media Guidelines

Many corporations have created employee guidelines for using social media on the job. Consider some essential guidelines:

▶ **Show respect.** Treat others with courtesy and respect.

▶ **Show responsibility.** Think before you communicate.

▶ **Demonstrate integrity.** Show sound moral character.

▶ **Be ethical.** Would your grandmother like what you're doing? If not, don't do it.

▶ **Add value.** Say something that moves the ball forward. Add to the conversation.

Fortunately, solutions to these challenges are starting to emerge. Corporations are developing social media guidelines for employees and training employees on proper and appropriate social media behavior.

This brings us to our final point, which deals with an organization's capability to achieve its desired brand positioning via social media. We would be very rich if we collected a dollar each time we heard a CMO confess to being unsure about investing in the resources required to adopt a social media strategy. So many of them hire interns from prestigious universities to help them "figure it out" and "determine the ROI" of such an investment—at least, that's been the norm in the most recent past. But hiring a few recent graduates to handle something as important as social media is a prescription for disaster, which is why we recommend assigning your social media program to a more seasoned employee or group of employees.

SOCIAL MEDIA ISN'T FREE

The bottom line is that any effort requires investment. Sometimes this is an investment in people. Sometimes it's an investment in technology. Often it simply boils down to an investment in time.

When you're thinking about how you can use social media to connect with your customers and, ultimately, make money, ask yourself these key questions:

▶ Will the benefits of engaging in social media marketing outweigh the risks? Are there any risks if you do participate?

▶ Does your industry, product, or brand have a unique characteristic that may make social media more or less critical and relevant?

- ▶ Can you use social media marketing to influence key stakeholders in the intended manner?

- ▶ Do you know which platforms will resonate best with your stakeholders, and can you motivate them to participate?

- ▶ Does your organization have the necessary capabilities—including resources and processes—to achieve your desired brand positioning through social media?

- ▶ Do you have a way to integrate social media into your current marketing communications strategy?

- ▶ Do you have a set of metrics that will help you understand whether the return from social media was worth the investment?

In asking these questions, you're taking one of the first important steps to growing your sales and revenue with a social media marketing campaign.

We've covered a lot of good ground designed to set you up for social media success. Let's revisit the key concepts and action steps and then move on to more good stuff.

- ▶ **Key concept:** The average tenure for a chief marketing officer is only 11 months.

- ▶ **Action step:** Avoid the fate of most CMOs by embracing the concept of running only social media programs that can be measured on an ROI basis.

- ▶ **Key concept:** Several basic formulas illustrate the impact marketing has on sales.

- ► **Action step:** Learn and understand the marketing mix formula outlined in this chapter. You'll be tested on it tomorrow. (We're kidding.)

- ► **Key concept:** Some larger corporations are adopting a "wait and see" approach to social media.

- ► **Action step:** If you "wait and see" too long, you give your competition an edge. Instead, adopt a set of social media guidelines for your company. (For examples of corporate social media guidelines, visit www.60SecondMarketer. com/SocialGuidelines.)

YOU WERE PROBABLY PRETTY FIRED UP WHEN SOCIAL MEDIA FIRST CAME ALONG. IT WAS AN EXCITING NEW APPROACH, A LOT OF BUZZ WAS CIRCULATING ABOUT IT, AND EVERYBODY WAS EAGER TO SEE IF SOCIAL MEDIA WAS GOING TO BE LIKE USING GOOGLE TO DO A PAID SEARCH CAMPAIGN. MAYBE YOU REMEMBER PAID SEARCH— IN THE EARLY YEARS, IT WAS SO SUCCESSFUL THAT IT WAS THE EQUIVALENT OF PRINTING MONEY. TODAY IT'S A SOLID, VIABLE MEDIUM, BUT IN THOSE EARLY YEARS, IT WAS *SUPER HOT*.

CHAPTER 6

WHY YOUR FIRST SOCIAL MEDIA CAMPAIGN DIDN'T WORK

That's what social media is today, super hot. But somewhere along the way, a lot of people have stumbled in using social media. They've launched a campaign, sometimes with great fanfare, and failed miserably.

In Chapter 2, "The Evolution of Marketing," we mentioned Red's Porch, the restaurant and bar that made one of the greatest offers of all time (free alcohol) to the first 100 people who followed it on Twitter. Unfortunately, the promotion didn't work. A number of factors contributed to the failure, but the main one was that Red's Porch did not have social media magnetism.

If your brand has social media magnetism, it's so powerful that people are attracted to it the way metal is attracted to a magnet. Your brand is so powerful that people will go out of their way to be affiliated and associated with your company, because it gives them a sense of style, cache, and panache.

For an example of this, check out MyStarbucksIdea.com. It's one of Starbucks' many social media campaigns, and it's a particularly good example of how Starbucks has leveraged people's passion about their coffee and turned it into brand loyalty. Brand loyalty is one of the components of social media magnetism. If you have it, as Starbucks does, you're golden.

The problem is, you're not Starbucks (unless, of course, you actually *are* Starbucks, in which case, we'd like to say, "Hello, Starbucks!").

Our point is, if you're a company that sells paper or pet supplies or, God forbid, industrial widgets (apologies to the industrial widget makers out there), you're going to have to reach out to consumers and engage them in your social media campaign.

How can you do this? By creating a campaign that gives consumers something valuable that they don't currently have. This can be giveaways and other relatively traditional special promotions. This also can be information that the visitor finds useful. Better still, this can be a tool that keeps the visitor coming back for more.

Money-Making Tip

You can download a list of effective and easy-to-implement social media promotions at www.60SecondMarketer.com/SocialPromotions.

One of the best and smartest versions of these tools comes from HubSpot, a Boston company. HubSpot realized that one of the best ways to create inbound traffic to its Web site was to create a tool that people couldn't do without. So the company created a search engine optimization (SEO) analysis tool called WebsiteGrader and put it up on its Web site.

What's an SEO analysis tool? It's a sophisticated program that analyzes how Google, Yahoo!, or Bing sees your site. The real stroke of genius was that the folks at HubSpot decided to include WebsiteGrader on the Web site. By sharing their tool with other people, they created inbound traffic, which ultimately converts to customers.

"A great way to get more customers using social media is not just to engage, but to *educate*," says HubSpot chief technology officer and founder Dharmesh Shah. "We believe in this passionately at HubSpot, and it has worked miracles for us. We've learned that the more people you *make smarter* by educating them, the more leads and customers you get."

So far, HubSpot's WebsiteGrader has generated grades on more than two million URLs. So on more than two million occasions, potential customers for HubSpot have visited, engaged with, and interacted with one of the tools on its site. That kind of traffic is mind-boggling, especially if you're a company with only a few hundred employees.

Check out MyStarbucksIdea.com or WebsiteGrader.com the next time you're at a computer. You'll get a clear sense of what they're doing to engage people—and keep them engaged—with their companies.

This brings us back to one of the key questions a lot of folks are asking themselves right now: "If social media is such a powerful tool, why did my first campaign fail?"

It's a great question. We analyzed the most common mistakes people make when they run a social media campaign and came up with the following list. Read through it and put a check mark by the ones that apply to you. Don't be surprised if you have more than one check mark—the idea is to figure out where you're coming up short so you can focus on fixing the problem areas:

❏ **You didn't measure the results of your campaign.**
Interestingly, this is an all-too-common problem. We
discuss ways you can measure the results of your next
campaign in an upcoming chapter.

❏ **You didn't set clear objectives.** Some companies create
a Facebook page or a YouTube channel before they think
through their objectives. Is it to build awareness? To drive
traffic to a landing page on their site? To give people a
channel to make comments and record their frustrations?

❏ **You thought social media was only about Twitter,
LinkedIn, Facebook, or YouTube.** Of course, social media
is about having many conversations across as many
platforms as you can manage. The more opportunities
you provide customers to engage with you, the more
successful your campaign will be.

❏ **You didn't know how to set up a landing page.** One basic
model of social media success looks like this: prospect →
social media channel → landing page on Web site → new
customer. If you don't have a landing page on your Web
site that's designed to convert prospects to customers, you
won't be able to track your return on investment (ROI).
No ROI, no social media campaign (or, rather, no *effective*
social media campaign).

❏ **You didn't remarket to customer prospects.** Most
prospects who visit your landing page won't become
customers. In fact, the vast majority won't. But that doesn't
mean they're never going to buy. It just means they aren't
going to buy at that time. Keep them in your pipeline—
you'll get them someday if you remarket to them.

❑ **You didn't know how to turn a social media campaign into a sales and marketing campaign.** Social media isn't just about building awareness. It's about turning prospects into customers. Don't be shy about nudging prospects along the sales funnel. They expect it, to a certain degree.

❑ **You sat on the sidelines.** True story: We were in contact with a creative director at a major advertising agency a while back who said, "This whole Internet thing is just a flash in the pan, and I can't wait for it to blow over." We're serious, he said that. Our point? You don't want to be that guy.

❑ **You downplayed the importance of social media.** Some people don't sit on the sidelines as much as they participate without passion. That's almost as bad as sitting on the sidelines. You don't want to be that guy, either.

❑ **You thought you could do social media in ten minutes a day.** Social media is a little like a marriage: You won't have a successful marriage if you plan on spending just ten minutes a day having a dialogue with your spouse. The same holds true for a successful social media campaign.

❑ **You thought social media was like traditional marketing.** Social media and traditional media have a lot of similarities. But they have a lot of differences, too. Your job is to embrace those differences. Don't be scared— social media won't hurt you.

We could go on and on about some of the ways your social media campaign might have failed, but we won't. Our job here

is to show you ways to succeed with social media, not how
to fail.

So we'll keep going. For now, let's review the key concepts and
action steps you should know from this chapter.

- ▶ **Key concept:** If you're not a social media magnet like Nike,
  Apple, or Harley-Davidson, customers won't automatically
  come to you. You have to set up campaigns that attract
  them.

- ▶ **Action step:** Download the list of the top social media
  promotional ideas at www.60SecondMarketer.com/
  SocialPromotions.

- ▶ **Key concept:** HubSpot and MyStarbucksIdea.com are two
  of the more successful models that companies are using to
  attract visitors to their Web sites.

- ▶ **Action step:** Visit both sites and study what makes these
  models successful. Use the sites as inspiration to do a
  bigger, better, bolder version of the same thing for your
  company.

- ▶ **Key concept:** Several common reasons explain why some
  social media campaigns don't work.

- ▶ **Action step:** Use our checklist to identify the areas you
  need to focus on in the future.

HAVE YOU EVER BEEN IN A SITUATION WHEN PEOPLE WERE SAYING NEGATIVE THINGS ABOUT YOU? MAYBE IT WAS IN THE LUNCHROOM IN MIDDLE SCHOOL OR AT A PARTY WHEN YOU WERE YOUNGER.

CHAPTER 7

MANAGING THE CONVERSATION

If you're like most of us, you probably ignored the people who were saying the negative things. You probably let them continue their gossip and just walked away from them.

But what if you had decided to join the conversation? What if you had decided to introduce yourself and talk to the other people? What if you had decided that, once they got to know you, they probably wouldn't feel so negatively about you? If you had just taken a few steps and talked to them, they might have gotten to know you better and might have even changed their opinion about you. Who knows? They might have even said some *positive* things about you.

The same holds true with social media. If people are saying negative things about your company online, you have two choices. The first is to ignore the conversation. The second is to participate in it.

What happens if you ignore the conversation? Before long, others join in the fray and things quickly spin out of control. You end up reacting to the conversation rather than controlling it. That's not good.

Research indicates that when someone has a positive experience with your brand, that person might tell one or two other people about the experience. But when someone has a negative experience with your brand, that person will tell 11 other people about the experience. It's hard to say how many of the 11 people will perpetuate the negative story, but it's safe to say that the "gossip" doesn't stop there. In all likelihood, an additional 10 or 15 people might hear the story from the original 11.

That's potentially 21 to 26 people who hear something negative about your brand, just based on one customer's less than stellar experience. But that research doesn't even factor in the power of the Internet, which can increase the effect tenfold or even a hundredfold.

Did You Know?

Information travels across the Internet at almost 186,000 miles per second. Given that, it's not surprising that consumers' perceptions about brands change more rapidly than ever.[1]

When Motrin ran a commercial about mothers who wear body-hugging slings for their children, several bloggers found it objectionable. Apparently, the bloggers felt that the spot took a swipe at mothers who have back pain as a result of wearing the baby slings. Messages like those seem to spread around the globe at the speed of light, so it wasn't long before the whole Motrin Moms commercial turned into the Motrin Moms fiasco.

A few days after the campaign launched, Motrin pulled the spot and issued a public apology. But an analysis conducted by Lightspeed Research found that almost 90 percent of the survey respondents had never seen the ad. When they did see it, about 45 percent liked it, 41 percent had no feelings about it, and only 15 percent didn't like it. Just 8 percent said it negatively affected their feelings about the brand, compared with 32 percent who said it made them like the brand more.

What happened? A handful of bloggers started a whirlwind of activity that resulted in so much negative content swirling around the Internet that Motrin had to cancel the spots—even though post-fiasco research indicated that the company didn't have to.

A similar incident happened to United Airlines when a musician named Dave Carroll uploaded his music video, called "United Breaks Guitars," to YouTube. Dave, who strikes us as a very nice and genuine guy, wrote the song after getting the brush-off from United when the company refused to pay for the guitar that some baggage handlers broke. Dave's first video generated more than eight million YouTube viewings.

According to U.K.'s *Times Online,* "within four days of the song going online, the gathering thunderclouds of bad PR caused United Airlines' stock price to suffer a mid-flight stall, and it plunged by 10 percent, costing shareholders $180 million. Which, incidentally, would have bought Carroll more than 51,000 replacement guitars."

Whether Dave Carroll's YouTube video really had anything to do with the stock price dropping 10 percent is arguable, but the hard fact is that more than eight million people now have a less than stellar impression of United Airlines.

It's easy to second-guess what United or Motrin should have done once things started spiraling out of control. But if they'd

both been more deeply engaged in the online conversation—
if they'd both gotten out ahead of the story—perhaps their
situations would have been different.

PARTICIPATING IN THE CONVERSATION

So where does all this lead us? Right back to where we
started: When you have a choice between participating in the
conversation or sitting on the sidelines, you should *always
participate in the conversation.* When you do so, you can help
frame the issues and spread correct information about your
brand or product.

Participating in or controlling the conversation is a little labor-
intensive, but sometimes you don't have a choice. We know
one brand (we'll call them Brand A) that spends more than $15
million a year on traditional advertising. They're sophisticated
marketers who track the results of every dollar they spend.
They even track the online chatter about their brand and their
competitor's brand online.

The problem is that Brand A is getting absolutely trashed
online. Seriously, people are writing terrible (and usually false)
things about their company. Worse still, people are confusing
Brand A with a competitor who actually *is* guilty of some
terrible things.

Yet here's the incredible part: Brand A has decided to sit on the sidelines and not participate in the conversation. What the ...? Really? Somehow these guys have decided that it's better to save their money than to invest it in reframing the online chatter that's damaging the long-term value of their brand. How's that for short-term, narrowly focused thinking?

So how do you manage the online conversation in such a way that people are exposed to accurate information about your brand? The starting point, of course, is to monitor the online chatter about your brand. You can use several companies to do this, including Techrigy and Nielsen BuzzMetrics. Here's a quick rundown of what these companies can measure:

- ▶ Online mentions across blogs, microblogs, message boards, wikis, social networks, video-sharing sites, and mainstream media

- ▶ Daily volume and trend analysis

- ▶ Word cloud analysis to show what words are being used in association with your brand (such as *cheap, free, valuable, love,* and *hate*)

- ▶ Word cloud analysis to show what words are being used in association with your competitor's brand

- ▶ Gender and age analysis of people describing your brand online

- ▶ Most active domains showing results for your brand (YouTube, Twitter, Wikipedia, and so on)

▶ Geographic distribution of posts, both nationally and internationally

▶ Positive and negative sentiment surrounding your brand

▶ Forum comment metrics

▶ Facebook Fan Page analytics and metrics

But gathering data is just part of the challenge. The real question is, what are you going to do with the data?

One approach is to use something BKV Digital and Direct Response calls i-Cubed system. BKV is a marketing communications firm that creates highly measurable marketing campaigns for brands such as AT&T, Six Flags, and the American Red Cross. It's also the primary sponsor of the *60 Second Marketer,* the online magazine run by Jamie Turner, one of the authors of this book.

When BKV saw the power and impact that social media was going to have on brands, it came up with the i-Cubed system:

▶ **Information** is all the data and statistics you can gather about your social media campaign. You can use several tools for this, in addition to the ones mentioned earlier, including Biz360, Radian6, Visible Technologies, and the old workhorse Google Analytics.

▶ **Insight** involves taking a deep dive into the data to explore patterns, spikes, relationships, and other information that you'll notice only after you've really digested the information. When you're investigating at this level, it's easy to get stuck in data overload, so don't be afraid to take a step back every once in a while and ask yourself, "Okay, I understand the data, but what does this mean in *human* terms? How can I translate this information into a story about my customers or prospects?"

▶ **Impact** is all about creating a campaign that leverages the information and insight and turns it into a specific, measurable, action-oriented program to drive revenue for your brand. If the data shows that long-form blog posts don't get much traffic, but your YouTube videos do, you'll want to leverage that insight into your campaign. (Of course, you'll want to go much deeper than that in your analysis, but you get our point.)

USING THE I-CUBED SYSTEM TO MANAGE THE ONLINE CONVERSATION

One client we've worked with used the i-Cubed system to manage the online conversation about its business. It's an interesting story and worth sharing because a lot of companies have probably had similar problems.

It all started about 15 years ago, when a product this company made malfunctioned. In almost all cases, the malfunction was the result of user error, but enough people were affected that lawsuits started flying around like a bunch of gnats on a summer evening. Instead of fighting the cases in court, the company decided to settle out of court.

The problem seemed to go away until, 15 years later, a little-known blogger decided to upload a poorly researched and inflammatory article post on his blog. The problem became pretty serious when Google ranked this post #2 on the first page of the search engine. The only site ranked higher than this blog post was the company's official Web site.

You can imagine the kinds of problems that raised for this company—a blogger with inaccurate information got ranked #2. When you're in that spot, it's very hard to knock it out of that position.

So what did we do? We used the i-Cubed system of Information, Insight, and Impact to develop a social media campaign that was designed to flood the Internet with accurate, transparent and helpful information about the company. We pulled out all the stops, using YouTube, LinkedIn, Twitter, Facebook, Flickr, and seven different blogs designed to ethically, honestly, and transparently provide accurate information about the company and its products.

What were the results? (Recall that the third *I* in the i-Cubed system is *Impact*.) The company dominated more than 65 percent of the conversation on the first page of Google. And by "dominate," we don't mean that the company flooded the Internet with sales pitches—that would have been counterproductive. Instead, it flooded the Internet with good, useful, and accurate information about its products and its industry.

Several key concepts in this chapter are worth keeping in mind. More importantly, you'll want to execute several action steps to keep moving forward with your next social media campaign.

- ▶ **Key concept:** You have two choices in social media: ignore the online conversations about your brand or participate in them.

- ▶ **Action step:** Choose to participate in the conversation. Be helpful, friendly, and, most of all, accurate.

- ▶ **Key concept:** Dozens of companies can help you gather data about the online chatter about your company.

- ▶ **Action step:** Start gathering data related to this chatter. Many of the resources have free entry-level versions.

- ▶ **Key concept:** The i-Cubed system is about information, insight, and impact.

- ▶ **Action step:** Make sure you follow this simple system in your next social media campaign. Gather information, develop insights, and measure the impact.

ENDNOTES

1. See www.fcc.gov/cgb/consumerfacts/highspeedinternet. html.

REMEMBER THE GAME SIX DEGREES OF SEPARATION? THE IDEA WAS THAT YOU COULD CONNECT ANY CHARACTER IN ANY MOVIE TO KEVIN BACON BY CONNECTING NO MORE THAN SIX ACTORS. THE GAME WAS BASED ON THE SMALL WORLD EXPERIMENT, CONDUCTED BY STANLEY MILGRAM, AN AMERICAN SOCIAL PSYCHOLOGIST WHO WAS FAMOUS FOR A VARIETY OF INTERESTING AND INNOVATIVE SOCIAL PSYCHOLOGY EXPERIMENTS.

CHAPTER 8

CREATING CIRCULAR MOMENTUM

The theory that we're all connected through six degrees of separation is true, in many cases. Oh, sure, it's not true if you're a member of the secluded Baniwa tribe in the Amazon Rainforest. But if you're Nanci Steveson living in Bay Head, New Jersey, the odds are pretty good that you could be connected to, say, Davis Tucker living in Austin, Texas, through no more than six degrees of separation.

That's important because it drives home the point that your product or service is linked to a lot of people who have had a positive (or negative) experience with it. The good news is that if people have a positive experience with your brand, they just might spread the word via social media. However, if people have negative experiences with your brand, the word gets out just as quickly.

We call this **circular momentum.** The idea behind circular momentum is to use social media to grow your brand's positive impression. When you tap into the power of circular momentum, you can let your brand advocates (those who love your product) do a lot of your marketing for you.

USING CIRCULAR MOMENTUM TO BUILD YOUR BRAND

You need to keep one important thing in mind when you're trying to use circular momentum to build a positive brand impression: transparency. If you're not 100 percent honest and transparent in your dealings with people on the Internet, you'll eventually be found out. And nobody likes to be outed on the Internet.

However, if you can create a positive experience for people on your social media channels, you'll be able to leverage circular momentum for the better.

Take Equifax as an example. Equifax is the oldest consumer credit reporting agency in the United States. It's safe to say that the company is somewhat conservative. Fortunately, two social media advocates were prepared to nudge Equifax into new territory. Jana Ferguson, who works at BKV Digital and Direct Response, and Helen Wanamaker, the vice president of marketing at Equifax Consumer Services, decided to push ahead into new and uncharted waters.

"We knew that Facebook was a place where our customer prospects congregated," said Helen. "We weren't sure, at first, how to tap into everything going on at Facebook. But after working through some initial thoughts and ideas, we realized the worst thing we could do was to do a hard sell. So we set everything up so that it was all about creating a community where people could come in, talk with other like-minded consumers, and even communicate directly with Equifax. Before long, we had more than 10,000 fans, with hundreds of them actively participating in the conversation."

Before launching the campaign, the team did extensive research to find out what the company's competitors were doing in the space. To their surprise and delight, its competitors, Experian and TransUnion, didn't have Facebook pages specifically branded to their companies. (Experian did have a Fan Page for FreeCreditReport.com, but it served more as a pop-culture tribute than as a service to consumers.)

The team also did research to find out what businesses outside of its competitive space were doing. They realized that many corporate Fan Pages were simply places where people vented their frustrations. To a certain extent, it's healthy and positive to give people a place to vent their frustrations. After all, research has indicated that after people can vent a little bit, they feel better about the companies they're frustrated with. It's also important to provide as much support and encouragement as possible so that you can minimize the frustration.

USING SOCIAL MEDIA FOR CUSTOMER SERVICE

In the case of Equifax, the company made sure that it responded quickly to complaints and, in the process, gave customers a sense that their frustrations were being addressed. This was the same approach that Frank Eliason used for his ComcastCares Twitter account. Eliason worked in customer service at Comcast Cable in Philadelphia. One day, he noticed some tweets about Comcast that angry customers had sent. Instead of sitting idly and watching the tweets fly by, Eliason reached out to the customers to see if he could help fix the problem. And customer service on Twitter was born.

The basic approach, practiced by @ComcastCares and scores of other companies, is to monitor the chatter happening on Twitter via Search.Twitter.com. By logging into Search.Twitter.com, you can see what people are saying about your products, your brands, or your competitors. When someone says something negative about your brand, you can reach out and try to rectify the problem.

That's what Eliason did at ComcastCares. In many cases, he gave people simple instructions to help them fix the problem (such as "Have you tried turning your modem on and off? Sometimes that fixes the problem."). Other times, he gave them e-mail addresses that had been set up to connect frustrated customers directly to customer service managers. In virtually all cases, customers were given the opportunity to connect with Comcast via Twitter, and that gave them the sense that things were being fixed.

Money Making Tip

Brands such as Southwest Airlines, Comcast, and Equifax are using social media for improved customer service. As a result, the brands have improved their customer retention rates, which helps justify the cost of some of their social media efforts.

Research has found that when humans feel as though they don't have control over a situation, they experience a high degree of stress. That's why people who work in environments where they have no control often freak out. But the same research indicates that when people have some sense of control over a situation, they feel less stress.

That's the dynamic Comcast and other companies that use Twitter for customer service are tapping into. By giving customers an outlet to vent, discuss, and even solve problems via Twitter, you're giving customers a sense of control. And when they have a sense of control, they feel better—about you, your brand, and your products and services.

SOCIAL MEDIA AS A RECRUITING TOOL

Ernst & Young is another company that has effectively used social media to create a community of followers. But instead of using it as a congregation point for customers and prospects the way Equifax has, the company uses it as a recruiting tool for future employees.

The rationale makes complete sense. People in their early 20s often use Facebook as a place to connect and collaborate. Ernst & Young decided to leverage this dynamic by creating a Fan Page that introduces Ernst & Young to prospective employees. Interestingly, the company doesn't use it to sell services or even to build relationships with future customers. Instead, it uses it to inform, involve, and inspire young people who might be good candidates for future employment.

The Big Idea

Companies don't always need to use social media as a sales tool.
They can also use it as a customer retention tool or a recruiting
tool.

The Ernst & Young Fan Page has more than 40,000 fans who ask
questions, start conversations, and generally stir things up with
Ernst & Young. Visitors can write on the wall, suggest the page
to friends, and even vote in polls that the company posts.

What does the company get in return? For starters, it's able
to answer questions that many young people have about
employment without tying up the phone lines of the company's
HR department. (Remember, Ernst & Young doesn't have to
answer each question every time—visitors can scroll down and
read responses to other people's questions. The net result is
that, instead of having to write one answer for every question,
Ernst & Young can write one answer that is read by several
people who have the same question. That's a more efficient use
of Ernst & Young's time and efforts.)

For some real fun and games, visit the Mini Cooper Web site at
MiniUSA.com. It's a site that not only loads incredibly quickly
(thank you, Mini Cooper gang), but also includes everything
from iPhone apps to viral videos that visitors can e-mail to
friends. The site is an excellent example of using a Web site as
a hub for a community to create a deeper relationship with the
brand.

What do all these companies have in common? What
philosophy do they all share about social media? It's quite

simple: They all know that the secret to a successful social media campaign is to use a hub-and-spoke system to create circular momentum across many channels (see Figure 8.1). Instead of seeing social media as something linear, they see it as something circular, interconnected, and viral.

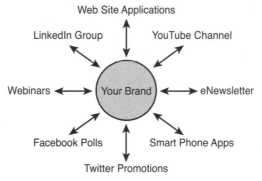

A Successful Campaign Creates Circular Momentum Across Many Platforms

Web Site Applications

LinkedIn Group

YouTube Channel

Webinars ⟷ Your Brand ⟷ eNewsletter

Facebook Polls

Smart Phone Apps

Twitter Promotions

Figure 8.1 A successful social media campaign uses a hub-and-spoke approach to have conversations across multiple platforms.

So when Equifax launches its Facebook Fan Page, it doesn't just sit in isolation. It's part of an ongoing marketing campaign that includes iPhone apps, YouTube videos, e-mail campaigns, online forums, direct response television, and a whole range of other touch points designed to engage, embrace, and enhance prospects' and customers' experiences with the brand.

The same holds true for Mini Cooper, Comcast, and Ernst & Young—all companies that have understood that the secret to a successful social media campaign is to create circular momentum across many platforms. When a dialogue starts on one channel, users can navigate to different channels to engage with the brand.

By providing multiple channels for users to talk with you, you let customers choose the channel they're most comfortable with. And by doing that, you increase the likelihood that they'll connect with your brand in any number of ways.

ARE YOU SET UP TO CREATE CIRCULAR MOMENTUM WITH YOUR SOCIAL MEDIA CAMPAIGN?

Let's take a quiz to find out if your social media campaign is set up to create circular momentum. The more times you can answer "yes," the more likely it is that you're setting up your social media campaign to leverage the power of circular momentum.

Answer "yes" to the questions that apply to you:

___ Do I understand that, in theory, all my customers and prospects are connected by no more than six degrees of separation?

___ Do I understand that a successful social media campaign runs across multiple channels?

___ Do I understand how circular momentum can help me supercharge my social media campaign across many platforms?

___ Am I prepared to engage customers who are venting their frustrations in a manner that will reflect positively on my brand?

___ Am I prepared to be 100 percent honest and transparent in my social media campaign, thus avoiding the risk of being outed on the Internet?

___ Am I prepared to respond quickly to customers and prospects who connect with me via social media?

___ Do I understand that the more channels I use in my social media campaign, the more opportunities I have to connect with customers and prospects?

If you answered "yes" to almost all these questions, then the likelihood of success remains high. If you answered "no" to almost all these questions, you can stop reading now and put the book away.

We're kidding about putting the book away. But you get our point: To successfully leverage a social media campaign, you have to communicate across a wide variety of channels. When you do this, you create circular momentum. And when you have circular momentum, the odds of growing your sales and revenue via social media grow exponentially.

Let's review the key concepts and action steps from this chapter.

▶ **Key concept:** Research indicates that most people are only six degrees of separation apart.

▶ **Action step:** Recognize that negative and positive comments about your brand circle the globe very rapidly.

▶ **Key concept:** Circular momentum is social media's version of the snowball effect.

▶ **Action step:** When you set yourself up to leverage the power of circular momentum, people who love your brand will do a lot of your marketing for you.

▶ **Key concept:** Circular momentum doesn't just happen; you have to help it along.

▶ **Action step:** Review the quiz questions in this chapter and work toward achieving as many "yes" answers as you can.

PART III

SOCIAL MEDIA PLATFORMS

SOCIAL MEDIA IS SIMILAR TO A SNOWBALL. WHEN IT GETS GOING, IT BUILDS AND BUILDS. WITH A LITTLE BIT OF LUCK AND A GOOD AMOUNT OF WORK, YOUR SOCIAL MEDIA CAMPAIGN WILL EVENTUALLY CREATE ITS OWN CIRCULAR MOMENTUM. WHEN THAT HAPPENS, YOU'RE OFF TO THE RACES.

CHAPTER 9

Social Media Is More Than Just YouTube, LinkedIn, Facebook, and Twitter

But most people misunderstand social media programs. It's not just about uploading a YouTube video or creating a LinkedIn profile. It's about creating a wide variety of channels through which your customers and prospects can connect with you.

The more channels you provide, the better the odds are that you'll create enough circular momentum to generate real results for your campaign. We like to think of it as analogous to a house fire. (It's an odd analogy, but hang with us.) If your house caught on fire, you'd have two choices: 1) use your garden hose to fight the fire, or 2) call the fire department and use dozens of serious fire hoses.

If you decided to use the garden hose to put out your house fire ... well, you might as well not even try. It won't work, so save your time and money. But if you decided to call the fire department, now you're talking. They can put some real effort behind the cause and, hopefully, save your house.

The bottom line is that momentum is critical, whether you're putting out a house fire or creating a social media campaign. Make sense?

The same holds true for a social media campaign. If your idea of a social media campaign is to create a Twitter profile and then update it every day or so, don't bother. It'll never get the traction you're looking for, so it's not worth it.

But if you're serious about setting yourself up for social media success, put some serious effort behind it. Add some depth and breadth to your social media campaign. **Depth** is diving deep into each social media platform and really putting some energy into it. **Breadth** is doing social media across a wide variety of platforms, not just one or two.

This raises the question of how much bandwidth you have for additional assignments at work. How can you add work to your already-full plate and expect to do a good job with it?

Well, here's some news. Despite what you've heard, social media isn't free. Although some of the media costs are free (for example, it's free to upload a video to YouTube), other costs, such as the production costs and the labor costs, aren't free. If you're a smaller business such as a restaurant or a real estate brokerage, that's an important consideration, because you shouldn't launch a social media campaign unless you have the bandwidth. If you work at a larger corporation, it's also an important consideration because you'll have to assign staff to manage it.

It's also important to really embrace the concept that social media is not just about uploading a YouTube video or creating a LinkedIn profile. Sure, those are important components of most social media campaigns, but those are not the *only* components of a social media campaign. A good, solid, viable social media campaign crosses many platforms and requires a commitment of time, money, and focus for it to succeed.

SOCIAL MEDIA TOOLS TO HELP YOU NETWORK, PROMOTE, AND SHARE

Okay, we've established that a good social media campaign is similar to a snowball that has the potential to build. We've also pointed out that a good social media campaign has depth (a serious, concerted effort behind it) and breadth (it extends across a wide variety of platforms). Now let's talk about the three broad categories of social media platforms—those that help you *network,* those that help you *promote*, and those that help you *share.*

Hundreds of different social media platforms exist, so we can't cover them all in this book. However, we can give you the most popular and relevant platforms that are part of each of these categories. By breaking them into categories, you can identify which tool is the most appropriate for your specific task.

You'll notice that you can apply some of the tools across several categories. For example, LinkedIn falls into the networking category, although it's often used to promote. For simplicity, we've assigned each tool to only one category.

We go into more depth on each of these tools in the upcoming chapters, but let's take a quick look at the tools that help you network. You can find a bunch of them if you look around, but the ones you're probably most familiar with include LinkedIn, Facebook, and Twitter. But the list doesn't stop there. Plaxo, XING, and Friendster are also great tools that you can use to connect with others on a professional (or more casual) level. Classmates and MyLife are tools that can help you find people who know you and see who's searching for you. Ning and Bebo are also excellent tools to help you create networks and share your life with others online.

Money-Making Tip

Social media isn't free. Both hard and soft costs are involved. It's important to include those costs in your metrics so that you can accurately measure your social media return on investment (ROI).

The social media tools that can help you *promote* are the tools that are often used for sales and marketing. You can use them to drive traffic to your Web site or to your social media channels. By doing so, you're using social media to do more than just build awareness—you're using it to drive revenue. And what's the point of doing anything in business if it doesn't ultimately drive revenue, right?

Some of the most well-known social media tools that you can use to help promote include YouTube, Flickr, and MySpace. Other great social media promotional tools include Picasa (photo sharing and editing), Xanga (blogging community), and iLike (similar to MySpace).

Using social media to promote your product or service is an art that we'll discuss in upcoming chapters, but realize that heavy-handed promotions can sometimes backfire. Social media is about *engagement* and *involvement.* The best ways to engage and involve a prospect or customer is to soft-sell—give them something useful that they can use that will ultimately seal your relationship with them for a future sale.

As with romance, you have to build trust and engagement first. After you've built up some trust and engagement over the course of several dinners and a few bottles of wine, you can take your date home to ... meet your parents.

Tools that help you *share* are just as important as tools that help you network or promote. Sharing is a key activity for social media practitioners. When you share (information, how-to tips, and insights), you're building a relationship. And over time, that relationship can evolve from one that's about sharing to one that's about commerce.

The most familiar sharing tools include Digg, Delicious, and StumbleUpon, which are all tools that people use to share articles, videos, and Web sites that users feel are worthy of their support. But social media sharing tools go beyond Digg, Delicious, and StumbleUpon. They also include SlideShare (presentation sharing), Scribd (document sharing), Wikipedia (information sharing), and Yelp (user-generated reviews).

The bottom line about sharing tools is that they're an important component in any social media campaign, but they also take more time to gain traction. It takes a lot of people to Digg an article on your blog before it rises to the top. Because of that, many marketers focus on networking and promoting platforms before they get deeply involved in sharing platforms.

WHAT TO USE WHEN

Another important consideration if you're diving deep into social media is which tools are more relevant for business use (as opposed to personal use) and which tools need to be updated most frequently (resulting in a greater time investment).

The handy 2×2 matrix in Figure 9.1 outlines this concept. For our purposes, we're assuming that you're using social media tools to drive revenue, not to chat with friends. You can get some perspective on the tools that are more professional versus more casual, and the tools that require frequent updates.

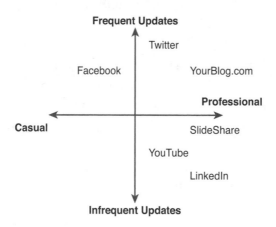

Figure 9.1   Using social media effectively involves understanding how to maximize the use of each platform.

LinkedIn doesn't require the kind of attention that Facebook requires, so you can "set it and forget it." Don't take that to mean you can forget about it for long stretches. It just means that you don't have to update it daily or hourly the way users update Facebook.

Twitter, of course, is the Mac Daddy of tools that require frequent updates. If you use it properly, you'll update it all day long, perhaps as many as 20–30 times a day. Remember, Twitter isn't about telling people that you're getting a cup of coffee or that the traffic was bad that morning. When used for our purposes, Twitter is about sharing information with your followers that they'll find helpful or useful. By sharing good information, you ensure that people will read and follow your tweets.

For our purposes, you can update YouTube whenever you have a new "how to" video to upload. Remember, the reason to use YouTube for business is to provide people with video information that they'll find useful. The best way to do this is to create videos that instruct and inform. With that in mind, you can update YouTube every week or every few weeks—whenever you have a new video to share.

Money-Making Tip

Data varies on this, but our experience indicates that search engines rank frequently updated blogs better than blogs that are updated infrequently. If you have a blog, be sure to update it two to five times a week.

If you have a corporate blog (and you should), you'll want to update it regularly. Uploading your best and smartest content to SlideShare is also an important and wise task.

With all this in mind, let's cover the key concepts from this chapter and the recommended action steps.

- ▶ **Key concept:** Social media is similar to a snowball that keeps building.

- ▶ **Action step:** Don't think that you can do social media in ten minutes a day. A good social media campaign is an ongoing effort that requires frequent attention.

- ▶ **Key concept:** Social media tools fall into three broad categories: those that help you network, those that help you promote, and those that help you share.

- ▶ **Action step:** Identify which platforms within each category will be most relevant to your prospects and customers. Make sure you use more than 1 or 2 platforms, but using more than 10 or 15 is probably overkill.

- ▶ **Key concept:** Some tools require frequent updating; others require infrequent updating.

- ▶ **Action step:** Be sure that you're aware of the workload associated with each tool before selecting it for your arsenal. Do a mental cost/benefit analysis of each tool before diving into it.

- ▶ **Key concept:** Some tools are more casual in nature; others are more professional.

▶ **Action step:** You want both casual and professional tools to be part of your social media campaign. A good balance of both gives prospects and customers a richer, more well-rounded experience with your brand.

YOU'RE A FARMER. THAT MIGHT COME AS A SURPRISE TO YOU, ESPECIALLY IF YOU'RE READING THIS FROM A LOFT IN NEW YORK CITY OR A CAFE IN LOS ANGELES. BUT THE TRUTH IS THAT ANYBODY IN BUSINESS, WHETHER IT'S A SERVICE BUSINESS OR A MANUFACTURING BUSINESS, IS ALSO IN THE BUSINESS OF *FARMING*.

CHAPTER 10

HOW TO USE NETWORKING PLATFORMS TO HELP YOU GROW YOUR SALES AND REVENUE

Why is this so? Because for any business to survive, it needs to have sales and revenues; and to have sales and revenues, you must have customers; and to have customers, you must have prospects.

How do you get prospects so that you can turn them into customers? We know of only one way: Plant the seeds of business today so that you can have a plentiful harvest tomorrow.

If you're a real estate agent, a restaurant owner, or an interior designer, you have to connect with people *today* so that you have customers *tomorrow.*

If you're an accountant, a lawyer, or a dentist, you have to connect with people *today* so that you have customers *tomorrow.*

If you're a Web designer, an architect, or a photographer, you have to connect with people *today* so that you have customers *tomorrow.*

If you sell cars, boats, motor homes, light fixtures, tools, food, knickknacks, clothing, or CDs, you have to connect with people *today* so that you have customers *tomorrow.*

If you're an entrepreneur, a CEO, a marketing coordinator, a salesperson, or a customer service agent, you have to connect with people *today* so that you have customers *tomorrow.*

The bottom line is that we all have to plant seeds today so that we can harvest the fruits of our labor tomorrow. And if we don't plant seeds on a consistent basis, we end up not having enough customers down the road.

Well, we have some good news. Social media is the perfect tool for people who understand that what you're doing today will influence your success tomorrow. It's a great way for businesses (such as yours) to build relationships with people who will buy your product in the future. And by nurturing those relationships now, you're ensuring that you'll have plenty of customers later.

WHO USES SOCIAL MEDIA?

How many businesses are using social media today so that they have customers tomorrow? According to the State of Social Media report from MarketingProfs, corporations who responded to the survey reported the following usage of the top social media sites:

- ▶ Corporate profile on Facebook: 48.2%

- ▶ Corporate Twitter account: 42.8%

- ▶ Corporate profile on LinkedIn: 39.1%

- ▶ YouTube presence to promote the company's products or services: 26.0%

- ▶ MySpace presence to promote the company's products or services: 8.0%

But research also indicates that individuals and businesses are taking a broader look at the variety of platforms that they can use to network via social media. As we've mentioned, social media is about more than just a handful of social media tools— it's about a broad range of tools all implemented within a well-thought-out strategy.

Let's take a closer look at some of the available networking platforms and the strengths and weaknesses of each. (Recall that we grouped social media platforms into three categories: those that help you *network,* those that help you *promote,* and those that help you *share.*) The list on the following pages is by no means exhaustive, but it should give you a sense of the top tools that are out there and how to use them for networking via social media.

Now let's assume that you're a businessperson who is interested in taking a step-by-step approach to using some of these tools to network with customers and prospects. You can find a step-by-step approach to this in Chapter 25 of this book, but let's assume that you're ready to dive in and that you want to get started right away.

Let's walk through a Quick Start Guide to using these social media networking tools to plant your business-development seeds today so that you can harvest them tomorrow (see p. 110).

Tool	Definition	Strengths	Weaknesses
Classmates	This easy, simple-to-use site helps you locate former classmates. Great for high school and college reunions.	A simple, uncluttered user interface makes it easy to use.	Because it's a site set up to connect former classmates, be cautious about using it for business purposes.
Facebook	Mark Zuckerberg started Facebook from his dorm room for his fellow students at Harvard. Today you can find everyone from toddlers to grandmothers on Facebook.	The site has been widely adopted by large segments of the population.	Will the younger generation stay on Facebook after Grandma has "friended" them?
Friendster	Here's a way to stay connected with everything that's important to you—hobbies, interests, causes, business, and so on.	A simple Web interface makes it easy to use.	The site is not as widely adopted as some other platforms and might have peaked.
hi5	This is a social networking platform that skews a little younger than Facebook. Members can play games, watch videos, flirt, give gifts, or just hang out.	It's a great alternative to MySpace or Facebook for the younger crowd.	It might not be the best social networking platform for business.
LinkedIn	This is the granddaddy of them all. LinkedIn has been around since 2003, which, in social media terms, is also known as "since the beginning of time."	Everybody's on LinkedIn.	Most people have trouble knowing what to do with LinkedIn after they upload their business information.
MyLife	This clean, simple site helps people connect with family, friends, and other relationships. MyLife boasts 750 million profiles.	The easy-to-use interface is one of the site's great strengths. It's perfect if you're looking for an engaging, simple way to connect with old friends.	It hasn't been as widely adopted as some other sites.

Ning	This site connects groups of people who are passionate about particular interests, topics, or hobbies. Marc Andreessen, who helped launch Netscape, cofounded this site.	Great for connecting with others who are interested in your area of expertise.	The user interface is so simple and uncluttered that getting started can be confusing. But after you've figured it out, it can be a good tool.
Plaxo	This site currently hosts address books for more than 40 million people. It helps people stay in touch with Pulse, a dashboard that lets you see what the people you know are sharing on the Web.	The graphical user interface makes it easy to use.	It hasn't been as widely adopted as some other platforms such as LinkedIn.
Twitter	This surprisingly successful tool has been widely adopted and is used for everything from business to fun and games.	Large segments of the population use Twitter.	It can be a distraction, especially if you have Attention Deficit Disor ... wow, look at that bird with all the pretty colors!
XING	XING has more than eight million subscribers worldwide. It has more than 34,000 specialized groups and more than 150,000 live networking events each year.	XING adds new developments to its platform on a regular basis.	It hasn't been as widely adopted as some other platforms, such as LinkedIn.

How to Use the Quick Start Guide

The steps outlined in this Quick Start Guide are a great way to dive into social media. But remember, a good social media campaign is executed with long-term goals in mind, not just short, quick hits such as these.

Step 1: Define your goals. Are you interested in driving traffic to your e-commerce site? Or are you interested in generating leads for your professional services business? Or perhaps you're interested in only building awareness for your organization? Figure all that out and then you're ready to move to Step 2.

Step 2: Get inside the mind of your customers and prospects. Don't launch any social media campaign without first thinking through why your customers and prospects are interested in connecting with you. What's in it for them? How is connecting with you in their best interest? What will they learn by connecting with you?

Step 3: Focus your initial energies on a handful of platforms. Start by putting a company profile on LinkedIn. Then create a Fan Page on Facebook. Follow that by creating a Twitter account. But don't do any of these things unless you will put some serious effort behind it. Don't create a Twitter account and ignore it—that's a waste of everybody's time.

Step 4: Drive people to your LinkedIn, Facebook, and Twitter channels. Remember, a social media channel is similar to a television channel—it's your specific connection to your "viewers." If you're going to drive people to your channels, make sure they have a reason to go there. Will they be able to get helpful information or a white paper? Will they be able to participate in a sweepstakes or a promotion? Will they be directed to a blog post that helps them in some way?

Step 5: Repeat Step 4. We're serious. Don't move on until you've repeated Step 4 and spent a good amount of energy driving people to your LinkedIn, Facebook, and Twitter channels.

Step 6: Upload content regularly. Now that you've driven an initial batch of people to your newly uploaded channels, you need to continuously update them with new and interesting information. Remember, your goal is to build a long-term relationship with your customers and prospects, so be sure to upload information that answers the "What's in it for me?" question.

Step 7: Keep your initial channels running while you explore other platforms. Don't move to other social networking channels until the first batch is running smoothly and you are continuously updating them. After that happens, you can shift gears and start exploring some of the other platforms that help you network. Remember, the key is to build (or rebuild) relationships with people before you start doing the hard sell. But when the relationship is established, you can say, "Did I mention that I sell insurance?" or "Have you seen our new e-commerce site that sells premium coffee?"

Let's recap some of the key concepts and action steps from this chapter.

▶ **Key concept:** It doesn't matter whether you sell cars, insurance, healthcare equipment, or pencils—everybody in business is a *farmer,* because we all have to plant seeds today to reap a bountiful harvest tomorrow.

▶ **Action step:** Embrace the concept of planting seeds today so you can grow your sales and revenues tomorrow.

▶ **Key concept:** Certain social media tools are specifically designed for networking. Some of these tools include LinkedIn, Facebook, and Twitter.

▶ **Action step:** Visit the Web sites of the social media networking tools that you're unfamiliar with (sites other than LinkedIn, Twitter, and Facebook). Go ahead, do it. It'll take only about five minutes to see what else is out there.

▶ **Key concept:** The social media networking Quick Start Guide outlined in this chapter gives you some ways to get started right away.

▶ **Action step:** If you're interested in jumping right in, go ahead and execute the Quick Start Guide in this chapter. But don't think that's all there is to it—a good social media program executes the campaign from a long-term, strategic standpoint. The Quick Start Guide is designed to get you up and running, but it's not the only thing you'll need to do for long-term success.

WHAT'S THE POINT OF SETTING UP, LAUNCHING, AND RUNNING A SOCIAL MEDIA CAMPAIGN IF YOU CAN'T USE IT TO PROMOTE YOUR PRODUCT OR SERVICE, RIGHT? AFTER ALL, THE BIG IDEA BEHIND SOCIAL MEDIA IS THAT YOU CAN USE IT TO CREATE RELATIONSHIPS WITH CUSTOMERS AND PROSPECTS TO GET THEM TO BUY MORE STUFF, FOR MORE MONEY, MORE FREQUENTLY.

CHAPER 11

How to Use Promoting Platforms to Help You Grow Your Sales and Revenue

With that in mind, let's take a look at the social media platforms that can help you promote your product or service. In the last chapter, we looked at the tools that can help you *network*. Now it's time to move on to the tools that can help you *promote* your brand.

Before we talk specifics, it might be a good idea to take a 30,000-foot view of the purpose of using social media to promote a product or service. The biggest mistake most people make is that they use social media the same way they've used traditional media. They think of social media as a tool designed to broadcast a monologue about a product or service. It's hard to believe that people are still using social media this way, but it's true.

The right way to use social media is to create a conversation with your prospects and customers. Conversations go back and forth, not just one-way. So if you use WordPress to create a blog about your company, you'll need to encourage people to engage with you by leaving comments, tweeting about your posts, writing articles on their own blogs about your posts, and doing other things that create the circular momentum and the snowball effect that we discussed in previous chapters.

Remember, the secret is to stir things up a bit. By stirring things up and generating buzz about your products and services, you're creating the kind of energy that snowballs into bigger and better things.

As we've mentioned previously, if we want you to remember one thing about using social media to promote your product or service, it's this: You want to create a dialogue, not a monologue.

Cool. Now let's keep going.

Let's take a quick look at some of the social media platforms that help you promote your product or service. This isn't an exhaustive list, but it'll help you get familiar with some of the better-known promotional tools under the social media umbrella.

That's a pretty straightforward review of the main platforms that you can use to promote products or services via social media. The most common question coming out of an overview such as this is, "I have only so many hours in a day. Which one of these should I dive into first?" See p. 121 for a Quick Start Guide.

Tool	Definition	Strengths	Weaknesses
Bing	Bing and its cousins Google and Yahoo! aren't technically social media platforms, but they are tools that you can use to promote your product or service, so we're including all three in this overview. The technique is the same for using any search engine to promote your product or service—you want to optimize your Web site with the right keywords so that the search engines see it. By doing so, you'll drive traffic to your Web site from the people doing searches on specific topics.	Bing uses "intelligent search" to make searches even more relevant for the user.	It's fighting against Google, which is a tough battle.
Blogging platforms	You can use these tools to create blogs. Some of them (such as Blogger, Tumblr, Vox, and Xanga) are straightforward platforms that are great for people who want to do a simple blog about their vacation, their company, or their family reunion. If you're ready to create a more robust blog that adds a lot of search engine optimizaton (SEO) value for your Web site, you'll want to use Joomla, Drupal, Typepad, or WordPress. Serious bloggers use these blogging platforms.	Blogs are one of the best ways for you to engage in a conversation with prospects and customers.	For blogs to be effective, you need to update them two to five times a week with good, helpful content.

Tool	Definition	Strengths	Weaknesses
Discussion boards and forums	Are you interested in creating an online forum where members of your community can engage with each other and offer each other advice? Then a discussion board or forum is for you. The best-known platforms for forums include Lefora, Zoho, Drupal, PhpBB, Simple Machines, Vanila, JavaBB, and vBulletin.	Forums are a great way to build a relationship with customers and prospects.	They require regular, ongoing time and energy to keep them running properly.
Google	Google isn't technically a social media platform, but you can use it as a social tool to drive visits to your well-optimized Web site.	It's easy to use and pervasive.	Is the company spreading its brand across too many channels? Does this confuse people? (Probably not, but we're struggling to come up with any weakness for Google. They're just so darn nice, it's hard to figure out what they're not good at.)
E-mail marketing	E-mail can often get overlooked in the world of social media, but if you define social media as tools that help you engage in a dialogue with your customers and prospects, then e-mail falls into the social media category. Popular e-mail marketing tools include Constant Contact, iContact, ExactTarget, and others.	E-mail is a highly measurable way to connect with customers and prospects.	E-mail marketing requires a concerted, ongoing effort if you want to do it right.

Flickr	You can use this photo-sharing site to build awareness and drive traffic to your product pages. If you're selling hunting rifles or tennis rackets or widgets, you can use Flickr to 1) build awareness for your product and 2) drive people from Flickr to your Web site.	Flickr is easy to use and has a clean user interface.	Photo-sharing sites are important, but they're not the first thing you should work on in your social media campaign.
Howcast	Wouldn't it be cool if you could visit a Web site where you could watch "how to" videos on the topic of your choice? Well, you can—it's called Howcast. It's an extremely worthy competitor to YouTube.	It's a great place to upload high-quality content.	The default is still YouTube. Most people are conditioned to automatically type "YouTube" into their browser.
iLike	If you're a musician, you'll want to upload your work to iLike, the dominant music application on a number of social media networking sites.	More than 50 million music lovers use iLike via Facebook, Orkut, iGoogle, and other platforms.	iLike is a crowded venue, which makes it difficult for musicians to break through.
iTunes	This isn't the only podcasting site, but it's the best known and most popular. If you're doing interviews with industry experts or you're creating mini-radio shows, iTunes is the place to be.	It's a well-known, well-respected platform.	If you don't create scintillating content, people won't come back for more.
MySpace	Ahhhh, MySpace. Arguably, this site started social media. Today MySpace is primarily used as a congregation point for younger people interested in pop culture. The platform is evolving and seems to be finding a niche.	It's a well-known social media platform that almost everybody has visited.	It's not the ubiquitous social media platform that it once was, simply because so many other social media platforms are clamoring for people's attention.

Tool	Definition	Strengths	Weaknesses
Picasa	This is a photo organizing, editing, and sharing site that Google owns. You can tag photos to enable quick searches by users.	As with most Google services, Picasa is easy to use and loads very quickly.	Photo sharing is important, but it's not the first thing that you should work on in your social media campaign.
Twitter	This surprisingly successful tool has been widely adopted and is used for everything from business to fun and games.	Large segments of the population use it.	It can be a distraction, especially if you have Attention Deficit Disor.... wow, two cardinals outside my window keep flying around in circles. How cool is that?
Vimeo	Think of Vimeo as a high-end YouTube. It's perfect for people who are interested in sharing their videos with a community of positive, encouraging, creative professionals.	You've gotta love a site that oozes upbeat, optimistic, life-affirming energy that Vimeo does.	It's not a default site the way YouTube is, but that might change in the near future.
Yahoo!	As with Google and Bing, this is not technically a social media platform. But it's a tool that ultimately can drive traffic to your Web site. Be sure to optimize your Web site so that search engines such as Yahoo! can see it.	Yahoo! is one of the workhorses of the search engine world, so it's always a good idea to keep it on your radar screen.	Is Yahoo! a search engine? An online portal? A Web magazine? Perhaps it's all these things. And perhaps that's not a weakness after all.
YouTube	YouTube is one of the better-known platforms used to promote businesses. The key to YouTube is to keep the videos short and sweet. Make sure they solve the "What's in it for me?" equation. YouTube is perfect for "how to" videos, but it's not a good place to upload the CEO's annual speech to shareholders.	YouTube is ubiquitous.	It's a cluttered environment that can sometimes have some pretty racy videos on it. (Or so we've heard.)

Quick Start Guide

We have another handy Quick Start Guide to help you dive right into the social media promotion world.

Step 1: Start by optimizing your existing Web site so that Google, Yahoo!, Bing, and other search engines can find it. Use Hubspot's WebsiteGrader.com tool to compare your Web site's visibility against your competitors' sites.

Step 2: Launch a blog. The best and easiest way to drive traffic to your site is to launch a blog. Make sure the blog is built inside your Web site. By using WordPress, Drupal, Joomla, or Typepad to build your blog inside your Web site, you'll get more link juice for your overall site.

Step 3: Upload new blog posts at least three times a week. Make sure your blog headlines and your title tags are phrases people are likely to search on so that you get visibility on search engines.

Step 4: Create an e-mail newsletter. Your customers and prospects want to be kept up-to-date on your latest special offers, right? Or they might want to read your white papers or articles that can help them with their businesses, correct? E-mail is one of the more important social media tools, and it's easy to implement. Don't ignore it.

Step 5: Upload content to Flickr, Picasa, discussion boards, forums, and other easy-to-use platforms. As part of our Quick Start program, you'll want to upload content and comments to these sites, but don't spend too much time here. You're just trying to get some initial juice from these platforms.

Step 6: Produce a short video. This doesn't have to be a top-notch, professional-quality video. It can be a basic video shot on a flip camera. The key is to provide content that's helpful and useful to your prospects and customers.

Step 7: Create a YouTube channel. Don't just upload your video to YouTube. Create your own channel so that you can customize the videos and the user experience.

Step 8: Upload your video to TubeMogul. This is a one-stop shop that distributes your video across many platforms, such as YouTube, Viddler, Howcast, Vimeo, Metacafe, and MySpace. It's a great time saver.

Step 9: Promote, promote, promote. Use traditional media, word-of-mouth media, social media, and any other technique you can think of to promote the heck out of your blog, your YouTube channel, and your e-mail newsletter. After all, what's the point of doing all that work if nobody knows you're out there?

Let's recap a few of the key concepts and action steps in this chapter.

- ▶ **Key concept:** Social media isn't similar to traditional media, because social media is about having a *dialogue*, not a *monologue.*

- ▶ **Action step:** Make sure all your social media campaigns are designed to build relationships with your customer prospects. Encourage comments, retweets, and Facebook posts.

▶ **Key concept:** Certain social media tools are great for promoting your products and services. These include user-generated videos, blogging, e-mail marketing, and other platforms mentioned in this chapter.

▶ **Action step:** Don't just talk about doing a video, a blog, an e-mail campaign, or any of the other tools described in this chapter—do it!

▶ **Key concept:** The social media promotion Quick Start Guide outlined in this chapter gives you some ways to get started right away.

▶ **Action step:** Go ahead and execute the Quick Start ideas in this chapter. They're a quick, easy way to jump into the world of social media.

IN THE PAST FEW CHAPTERS, WE'VE LOOKED AT SOCIAL MEDIA PLATFORMS THAT CAN HELP YOU *NETWORK* AND PLATFORMS THAT CAN HELP YOU *PROMOTE*. NOW WE LOOK AT SOCIAL MEDIA PLATFORMS THAT CAN HELP YOU *SHARE* INFORMATION ABOUT YOUR PRODUCTS AND SERVICES.

CHAPTER 12

HOW TO USE SHARING PLATFORMS TO HELP YOU GROW YOUR SALES AND REVENUE

Before we dive into the specific sharing platforms, let's talk about what it actually means to share. We've already talked about the danger of overpromoting with your social media campaign. We mentioned that doing the hard-sell using social media is usually counterproductive.

The reason for this is that social media is viewed (consciously or subconsciously) as a free tool on the Internet. In other words, people see blogs, forums, and communities as part of a web of interconnected dialogues that aren't necessarily intended for commerce.

Sure, people use the Web for commerce, but in many cases, people launch their Web browser without the intent of buying anything. Therefore, they resent people who come on too strong with a sales pitch. They consider the social media world a safe haven from marketers and corporations trying to sell products and services.

Money-Making Tip

People buy from you for only four reasons: 1) price, 2) service, 3) quality, and/or 4) exclusivity. Keep this simple truth in mind as you develop all your marketing campaigns, regardless of whether they're social media oriented.

Imagine that you're at a summer cocktail party. You've got a glass of wine in your hand, the breeze is blowing, and burgers and hot dogs are on the grill. Now imagine that someone walks over to you to strike up a conversation. That's harmless enough. But you'd be offended if the first thing out of their mouth was,

"I've got a special deal on a sports cars right now. Let's talk monthly payments."

The same holds true for most (but not all) social media campaigns. In most cases, the last thing you want to do is to start selling right away. The first thing you want to do is to start a conversation, to get to know the person and connect in a meaningful way.

We talked previously about how you want to approach social media as you do dating. You don't ask someone to come home with you on your first date (unless you're a drunk college student on spring break). Instead, you ask your date questions about her interests and hobbies. If all goes well, at the end of the date, you ask her out for a second date. On the second date, you get to know her better and ask more personal questions. This, of course, leads to a relationship that, hopefully, moves to a third date, then a fourth, then … twins!

We're kidding about the twins thing, but you get our point. Social media and dating are very similar. The idea is to build a lasting, trusting relationship that will result in some sort of fulfilling interaction.

Given all that, let's take a look at social media platforms that you can use to share information about your product or service. Remember, these sharing platforms are designed to provide helpful tools, tips, or techniques to your prospects and customers. In other words, they're not necessarily used for the hard sell. They're best for building awareness, interest, and desire for your product or service. If you play your cards right, that will ultimately result in a business transaction.

Let's take a look at these platforms.

Tool	Definition	Strengths	Weaknesses
Crowdstorm	If you want to get the inside scoop on digital cameras, DVD players, televisions, or other products, Crowdstorm is for you. The Crowdstorm community is built around the idea that when people share information about products, everybody benefits.	An easy-to-use Web site leverages the power of ratings and reviews for the benefit of users.	Because the site crowdsources reviews, it's not necessarily an effective tool for marketers. But it's always good to check with sites such as this one to see how your product is being perceived in the marketplace.
Delicious	Yahoo! owns this social bookmarking service. When someone tags your article, video, or blog post with a Delicious bookmark, it's the equivalent of a "vote." The more votes you get, the more visibility your content has on the Delicious Web site.	It's everywhere.	You need a lot of traffic and a lot of votes to show up on the radar screen.
Digg	This platform is similar to Delicious, in that people vote for articles, videos, and blog posts that they like. If your content gets enough Diggs, it's promoted to the front page, for millions of visitors to see.	As with Delicious, Digg is everywhere.	You need a lot of traffic and a lot of votes to show up on the radar screen.

Tool	Definition	Strengths	Weaknesses
Feedback	This is a social media platform that allows people to provide useful information to companies as diverse as Starbucks and Chipotle. Members of the Feedback community can read reviews and make additional comments.	It's an innovative use of crowdsourcing for information.	Because the site crowdsources reviews, it's not necessarily an effective tool for marketers. But it's always good to check with sites such as this one to see how your product is being perceived in the marketplace.
HootSuite	This tool enables you to manage multiple social media channels through one dashboard. If you have a company with more than one contributor to your social media program, HootSuite is a good solution.	The interface is easy to use. Setup is simple, yet it's still powerful.	If your social media program is no more extensive than updating a Twitter account, HootSuite is overkill.
Reddit	Similar to Digg and Delicious, Reddit is a source for what's new and popular on the Web. Users can vote articles up or down on the site, so readers can check out the hot, trending topics from blogs, newspapers, and other sources around the globe.	Along with Digg and Delicious, Reddit is everywhere.	You need a lot of traffic and a lot of votes to show up on the radar screen.
Scribd	This is the largest social publishing and reading site in the world. You simply upload your speech, e-book, or PowerPoint presentation to the site to awe others with your wisdom and expertise.	It's a great way to potentially get your content in front of thousands of readers.	A lot of other people are competing for the same eyeballs.

SlideShare	This is one of the better-known places to upload your content for sharing with others. You can share your PowerPoint presentation, e-book, podcast, or just about any other content with the SlideShare community.	As with Scribd, SlideShare is a great way to get in front of a large number of visitors. A lot of other people are competing for the same eyeballs.	There are a lot of other people competing for the same eyeballs.
StumbleUpon	This platform is similar to Digg, Delicious, and Reddit. When you rate a Web site that you like using StumbleUpon, you automatically share it with like-minded people. It also helps you find great sites your friends recommend.	StumbleUpon helps get your content to people who aren't regularly exposed to your products or services.	It competes with several other well-established tools, including Digg, Delicious, and Reddit.
TweetDeck	Similar to HootSuite, TweetDeck provides a way to track many of your social media channels on one dashboard. It can be a time saver and a productivity enhancer, assuming that you're not easily distracted.	It's easy to set up and get started.	As with all dashboard tools, it can lead to distractions for employees who are easily ... Whoa! Is that a fly on the ceiling or just a speck of dust?

Tool	Definition	Strengths	Weaknesses
Wikipedia	It still amazes us that this user-generated encyclopedia is run by just a few dozen employees (along with hundreds of thousands of contributors around the globe). It's a great tool for legitimate entries. Don't try to game the system by adding overly promotional posts, but if your entry will be helpful to the Wikipedia community at large, have at it.	It's a great tool for uploading legitimate, helpful content about your product, service, or company.	If your target market is over the age of 40, they might struggle with Wikipedia's miniscule type.
Yelp	This platform offers user-generated reviews on cool places to eat, shop, drink, relax, and play. Yelp has an augmented reality smart phone application that makes using it on the run a blast.	User-generated reviews are a great way for customers and prospects to find out about your business.	Some people try to game the system with fake reviews, but Yelp does a pretty good job of keeping those fake reviews at bay.

A QUICK START GUIDE FOR SHARING PLATFORMS

Okay, that should give you a sense of the social media sharing platforms that are available to you. This isn't a complete list, but it should give you a quick overview.

So where do we go now? What can you do with all this information?

That's a bit of a challenge. The networking and promotional tools we mentioned previously are a little simpler to use and easier to get up and running. But as Kyle Wegner, a social media specialist at digital and direct response agency BKV, said, "You can't get 100 bookmarks until you get the first bookmark, so you might as well get started." It's sage advice, especially coming from a young person who can hardly grow a beard.

Quick Start Guide

Let's take a spin through a Quick Start Guide for social media sharing tools.

Step 1: Add social bookmarking capabilities to your blog and your Web site. You don't want to add this capability to every page on your site—just the ones that have content that you want shared with the world-at-large.

Step 2: Upload content to Scribd, StumbleUpon, and other content-sharing sites. By sharing information with others, you build awareness for you, your brand, and your company.

Step 3: Start using HootSuite, TweetDeck, or any other social media dashboard to manage your Twitter, Facebook, and LinkedIn accounts. These tools can effectively manage conversations across a variety of channels.

Step 4: Continuously add content that others will pick up. This includes writing blog posts that will provide helpful information to your prospects. It also includes creating enough buzz throughout your social media campaign to get picked up and seen by others.

If you follow the steps outlined in this chapter's Quick Start Guide, you should be able to gain some serious traction on the social media sharing side of the equation.

Okay, let's take a quick look at the key concepts and action steps from this chapter.

- ▶ **Key concept:** The Internet isn't a great place for the hard sell. People don't expect a hard sell online, and they resist companies or individuals who play that game.

- ▶ **Action step:** Practice the soft sell in just about everything you do online. Build trust and awareness first and then let the customer come to you, not the other way around.

- ▶ **Key concept:** Social media *sharing* platforms are good places to build awareness for your company. They're not necessarily effective channels for converting customers. Typically, that's done elsewhere, such as the landing page on your Web site.

▶ **Action step:** Use social media sharing platforms as awareness-building tools, not necessarily as direct-selling tools.

▶ **Key concept:** Social media sharing tools require regular, ongoing maintenance.

▶ **Action step:** You can't "set it and forget it" with social media sharing tools. You need to update content regularly so that you continuously build awareness for your product or service.

WE'VE COVERED A LOT OF
GROUND IN THE PREVIOUS
CHAPTERS. A LOT OF
THE INFORMATION WE'VE
INTRODUCED IS DESIGNED TO
GIVE YOU A CLEAR SENSE OF
THE SOCIAL MEDIA LANDSCAPE.
AFTER ALL, THE BEST WAY TO
DEVELOP A STRATEGIC SOCIAL
MEDIA PROGRAM IS TO STEP
BACK AND LOOK AT THE PLAYING
FIELD BEFORE YOU DEVELOP
YOUR PROGRAM.

CHAPTER 13

MOBILE MEDIA, AUGMENTED
REALITY, AND WIDGETS, OH MY!

Before we go on, it's a good idea to recap a few of the concepts we've addressed so far.

A QUICK REVIEW

For starters, recall that social media is divided into three different categories: the medium, the platform, and the channel.

The medium is the broad category of technologies that provide a way for consumers and companies to have a digital dialogue. An example of a medium is a user-generated video or a blog. A platform is a specific tool that is used within a medium. So to take our example further, YouTube is a platform that falls under the user-generated video medium, and WordPress is a platform that falls under the blog medium. A channel is a specific vehicle that uses the platform to distribute its message. The YouTube channel for the 60 Second Marketer is www.YouTube.com/60SecondMarketer. The blog channel for the 60 Second Marketer is www.60SecondMarketer.com/blog.

In previous chapters, we looked at the different platforms you can use to connect with customers and prospects. They weren't exhaustive lists, but they were lists that gave you a sense of the different kinds of tools you could use to network, promote, and share.

Platforms that help you network include LinkedIn, Facebook, and Ning. They're primarily used by people who want to connect with other people, although plenty of companies and organizations are now using them to connect *brands* with other people.

Platforms that help you promote include e-mail platforms such as Constant Contact, blogging platforms such as WordPress, and search engine platforms such as Google. Companies, organizations, and individuals often use them to build awareness and drive sales for their brands.

The Big Idea

Grouping social media tools into categories makes it easier to wrap your mind around them. Here's a reminder of what a medium, a platform, and a channel are:

▶ Medium: User-generated video

▶ Platform: YouTube

▶ Channel: YouTube.com/60SecondMarketer

Platforms that help you share include Delicious, Digg, and HootSuite. Companies, organizations, and individuals use them to share information with others. For our purposes, we recommend using them to build awareness and drive sales, but plenty of people use them just to share information (and there's nothing wrong with that).

Okay, let's keep moving.

MOBILE MEDIA OVERVIEW

One of the more important tools used in social media right now is mobile media. Some people say that mobile media isn't a social media tool at all, but because it's a tool that allows brands and customers to have a digital dialogue, we're including it in the mix.

Let's start by looking at how people are using mobile media. According to the Mobile Marketing Association, people interact with mobile media in 12 ways:

- **Click to call**—Users place an outgoing call to the content provider or advertiser.

- **Click to locate**—Users find the closest business enabled by location-based services.

- **Click to order brochure**—Users receive marketing materials by supplying their postal addresses.

- **Click to enter competition**—Users enter text or sweepstakes to win prizes.

- **Click to receive e-mail**—Users receive an e-mail and a link to an online site by supplying their e-mail addresses.

- **Click to receive mobile coupon**—Users receive an electronic coupon on their mobile phone that they can redeem immediately at a participating merchant.

- **Click to buy**—Users make a purchase by paying with a credit card, adding the cost to their monthly mobile bill, or using some other form of mobile payment.

▶ **Click to download content**—Users download content, including logos, wallpapers, or ring tones, to their mobile phones.

▶ **Click to enter branded mobile Web site**—Users click a banner to get connected to a standing or campaign-specific Mobile Web site.

▶ **Click to forward content**—Users forward relevant content to friends, creating a viral campaign effect.

▶ **Click to video**—Users click a banner to view an advertiser's commercial for a product or service.

▶ **Click to vote**—Users reply to a ballot or poll from their mobile phone and provide marketers and brands with valuable research insights.

Did You Know?

Many countries, particularly in the developing world, are now bypassing the installation of landlines and going straight to mobile.

These are the 12 most common ways people use mobile media. And with the advent of smart phones, the use of mobile media to connect with customers and prospects will continue to explode. It's the perfect tool to create a digital dialogue with customers because they essentially have a mini-computer in their hands that facilitates geolocation for the companies that want to connect with them. Assuming that the customer or prospect has opted in for communication from the brand, companies can send real-time information to users based on their location and their preferences for communication.

HOW TO USE MOBILE MEDIA FOR YOUR BRAND

What are some of the primary ways in which brands are using mobile media to connect with customers and prospects? Companies are using six key approaches:

1. **Short Message Service (SMS)**—Nielsen estimates that SMS, usually referred to as texting, is the most common phone-based activity among U.S. cellphone users of all ages. That said, SMS for marketing purposes is equivalent to Mobile Media 1.0. Although SMS is still used frequently for marketing purposes, the wide adoption of smart phone technology will soon overwhelm SMS as a marketing tool.

2. **Mobile Web sites**—The most sophisticated marketers have a subdomain set up specifically for mobile phones. So, for example, when users type www.ESPN.com into a smart phone, the ESPN site actually figures out that they're visiting the site from a mobile device and redirects them to a subdomain (such as www.m.ESPN.com). That way, the user experience from a mobile phone is different than the user experience at a computer. The trick here is to be sure you create a mobile site that loads quickly and provides a simple, streamlined experience.

3. **Mobile ads**—Research indicates that mobile ads perform about five times better than Internet ads. The most common mobile ads are simple text links and graphical banner and display ads. Banner and display ads are sold based on cost per click (CPC), cost per acquisition (CPA), and cost per thousand (CPM). With CPC, you're charged only when someone clicks on your ad. It's the same model that a paid search campaign on Google, Bing, or Yahoo! uses. With CPA, you get charged each time you acquire a lead from your mobile media ad. CPA programs are great if you know how much a lead is worth to your company and what percentage of leads you can convert to a sale. With CPM, you're charged based on the number of times your ad is served. Typical rates for a CPM program are about $6 to $20 per thousand times your ad is delivered to a mobile device.

4. **Bluetooth marketing**—This is a form of on-demand mobile marketing that targets users based on precise geographical location. For example, if you're standing within 100 feet of Joe's Pizza, you might receive a free coupon, wallpaper, ringtone, or video or audio file that prompts you to visit Joe's and order a pizza. (Might we suggest a double pepperoni on thin crust?)

Did You Know?

In the United Kingdom, police departments are using mobile Bluetooth technology to communicate urgent messages to local communities.

5. **Smart phone apps**—The primary smart phone platforms include iPhone, Android, Palm, and Blackberry. The best way to use apps for marketing is to create something that's functional (such as a calculator), that's entertaining (such as a game), or that provides some sort of social connectedness (such as an app just for your community). Many applications are fee based, but companies are increasingly giving away smart phone apps as a way to stay connected with customers and prospects.

6. **QR codes**—These are the two dimensional barcodes that can be found in print ads, in-store posters, and even on the jacket cover of this book. They were initially used for tracking parts for vehicle manufacturers, but are now used in magazines, newspapers, signs and even T-shirts to send people to a Web page, download an MP3, dial a telephone number, or send an email message. Some people are even putting them on business cards so people can download contact information directly into their contact database.

AUGMENTED REALITY

Augmented reality (AR) is a medium that uses current technology to build new relationships with brands, customers, and prospects. AR superimposes virtual graphics on top of real-life objects on a computer screen or a smart phone. If you watch the Olympics on TV, you're experiencing AR when graphics, data, and other information are superimposed on the live footage of events.

For our purposes, AR is much more interesting than simply how it's used for sporting events. On smart phones and computers, AR is much more robust and interactive. For example, you can download an AR application from Yelp that allows you to look at a street through your viewfinder and see small balloons pointing out restaurants, with user-generated reviews of each one.

The Yelp application is particularly useful for people who travel a lot. Imagine standing on a street corner in an unfamiliar city and wanting to see if any good Thai restaurants are within walking distance. With Yelp, you can just hold up your smart phone and take a look down the street to see if there's a curried coconut chicken dish with your name on it around the corner.

Other companies that use augmented reality include Sorso Tea, IKEA, and Molson Dry Beer. Sorso Tea uses AR to engage customers and prospects at the point-of-purchase. Customers who are interested in Sorso Tea can hold a box of tea in front of the kiosk and see themselves in a virtual setting enjoying a cup of tea. IKEA, the Swedish furniture store, uses AR in Germany to get prospects to try out new furniture at home. Prospects simply aim their Web cam at the current furniture in their home to see an IKEA piece of furniture superimposed over the real furniture in the prospect's home. Molson Dry Beer allows customers to hold the bottle itself up to a computer screen to see an animated 3D party message. Users can even save their 3D experience and upload it to the Molson site to be viewed by others.

WIDGETS

Widgets are another tool marketers have turned to in an effort to improve the customer–company connection. A widget is a small application that can be downloaded and executed within a separate HTML-based Web page. Widgets include buttons, dialog boxes, pop-up windows, pull-down menus, and more.

Widgets come in three categories:

1. **Accessory widgets**—These are self-contained programs that don't require outside support to function. Examples include clocks, timers, calculators, and note takers easily accessible on a computer desktop.

2. **Application widgets**—These enhance an application by providing a less-complicated and often read-only interface. The iTunes controller and Address Book widgets fall into this category.

3. **Information widgets**—These are designed to work with data from the Internet. They allow you to monitor external events such as the weather, flight status, or stock prices.

Did You Know?

Use the ideas in this chapter as thought-starters for brainstorming sessions. By using these concepts as a starting point, you can create new and innovative marketing programs that will grow your sales and revenue tomorrow.

The primary purpose of a widget is to create customer and prospect interaction. Few widgets are transaction oriented, so don't think of a widget as a tool to drive revenue as much as a tool to create interest and demand for your product or service.

We've covered a lot of ground in this chapter, too. Let's recap it all with some key concepts and action steps.

- ▶ **Key concept:** People interact with mobile media in 12 different ways, including click to vote, click to video, and click to forward.

- ▶ **Action step:** Review each of the 12 approaches outlined in this chapter and see if you can come up with applications for your product or service. Do a cost/benefit analysis on the best three ideas to see if they're realistic ways to generate revenue.

- ▶ **Key concept:** Five different kinds of mobile applications exist: Short Messaging Service (SMS), mobile advertising, mobile Web sites, smart phone applications, and Bluetooth marketing.

- ▶ **Action step:** Review each of these five approaches and see if you can come up with applications for your product or service. Do a cost/benefit analysis on the best ideas to see if they're realistic ways for you to generate revenue.

- ▶ **Key concept:** Augmented Reality (AR) and widgets are two additional platforms marketers are using to engage with customers and prospects.

- ▶ **Action step:** Brainstorm ways you can use AR and widgets to grow your sales and revenue. Remember, today's brainstorms can be tomorrow's sales and revenue.

PART IV

SOCIAL MEDIA INTEGRATION

WHAT DO GEICO AND THE SHANE COMPANY HAVE IN COMMON? THEY'RE ALL WELL-KNOWN BRANDS THAT HAVE MADE THEIR MARK WITH CLEVER, CATCHY ADVERTISEMENTS. BUT THEY ALSO SHARE A LESS FLATTERING ACCOLADE THAT BINDS THEM TOGETHER: THEY HAVE LARGELY FAILED TO INTEGRATE THEIR COMMUNICATIONS CAMPAIGNS WITH STRONG, LONG-LASTING BRAND MESSAGES THAT RESONATE WITH CUSTOMERS OVER TIME.

CHAPTER 14

How to Integrate Social Media into Your Marketing Plan

Tom Shane's commercial narrations for The Shane Company, his chain of jewelry stores, left people wondering whether the brand could truly deliver on its promise to be their "friend in the diamond business." It wasn't until people actually went to the stores that they believed the premise: a store full of friendly, knowledgeable salespeople selling one-of-a-kind pieces at a good value. If you just relied on Tom's voice, you might not even wander into a store. And that's perhaps one of the reasons the company filed for bankruptcy protection.

Money-Making Tip

Don't confuse a marketing campaign's popularity with its actual success. For a campaign to be truly successful, it has to be popular with consumers *and* make the cash register ring.

Sure, Geico has the lizard. And some love the lizard. But they also have the cavemen, the B-list celebrities versus real people, good news versus bad news vignettes, talking pot holes and parking lot columns, stacks of money with googly eyes, and a narrating spokesperson who reveals "truths" that are hard to believe. Who are they trying to reach? What's the Geico brand message? What if I don't like lizards? While Geico is certainly gaining people's attention, they have a lot of churn, which means that customers who buy their insurance often switch to another insurance company a short time later.

So even though their TV commercials may have been memorable, both Geico and The Shane Company have struggled to retain customers over time. And isn't that the main goal of any marketing effort? It's not just about acquiring customers; it's about keeping customers loyal to your brand. Similar to a master chef who has a long waiting list for his restaurant, a successful marketer has to be skilled in mixing the marketing elements—product, price, place, and promotion—in such a way that customers keep coming back for more.

After all, consumers' perceptions of a company or a brand are the synthesis of a bundle of messages received via ads, packaging, direct marketing efforts, publicity, word-of-mouth, sales promotions, point-of-purchase displays, and even the type of store where a brand is sold. Most of these are marketer-generated, brand-oriented communications. Add to that all the conversations happening in the social media area. Clearly, brand messages can become garbled, diluted, or wrongly interpreted if they are being developed and disseminated in silos.

THE ADVENT OF INTEGRATED MARKETING COMMUNICATIONS

During the early 1990s, companies began to realize the need for more integration across all of their promotion tools. These firms began moving toward *integrated marketing communications* (IMC), which involves making your marketing communications consistent, coordinated, and synergistic by ensuring that you're speaking with one voice across all communications platforms. You want to be sure that what the consumer sees and hears isn't a bunch of unrelated, confusing, and mixed messages.

A few other factors were driving the push toward more integration:

- ▶ Marketers were under pressure to show a return on their marketing dollars invested. Others in the organization felt that traditional media advertising had become too expensive and wasn't cost-effective.

- ▶ Media fragmentation had resulted in more emphasis on targeted media and less emphasis on mass media.

- ▶ Power was shifting from manufacturers to retailers, who had more information about end users. Many marketers shifted their focus to promotional tools, such as sales promotions, that could produce short-term results.

As marketers embraced the concept of IMC, they began to ask their ad agencies to coordinate the use of a variety of promotional tools such as public relations (PR), sales promotions, direct marketing, Internet, and traditional media advertising.

Now we're seeing the need for integration all over again. Marketing executives are struggling to figure out how to keep their agencies coordinated as a slew of specialized digital agencies vie for their attention. In the midst of an economic recession, marketers face the daunting task of having to prove their worth.

Moreover, today's efforts to integrate across the various marketing disciplines are much more complex, given the rapid advances in digital platforms and explosive proliferation of user-generated content. New communications and information technology compete with existing traditional communications forms. So integration is not just needed across existing media forms; it's also needed across *old and new media forms.*

Don Schultz, Professor Emeritus at the Medill School of Communications at Northwestern University, developed a framework to illustrate today's marketplace as one of "push" and "pull" (see Figure 14.1). Marketers continue to push their communications out to customers and prospects through traditional forms such as TV, newspapers, magazines, radio, outdoor advertising, sales promotion, and PR. At the same time, customers have the ability to access, or pull, information from the marketer and the marketplace.

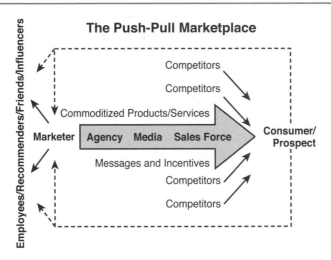

Figure 14.1   This framework, developed by Don Shultz at Northwestern University, illustrates the push–pull marketplace.

The primary change these new pull systems create is that customers are engaging in conversations about companies and brands around the world often without the knowledge of the marketer. Control over communications has changed hands. What was once the sole domain of the marketer, to push out carefully designed communications about companies and brands, has now become the domain of all the players in the value chain.

THE NEW WORLD OF MARKETING

In this new world of push-and-pull marketing, marketers no longer have the power to simply push out specific messages. Aligning and integrating both push and pull communication formats is vital to success.

Given all that, who is ultimately responsible for managing integration, a business client or its marketing agency? Lead agencies bundled together with support agencies under large holding company umbrellas claim they should be in charge of integration. But clients believe that *they* should be in charge.

In a recent Forrester study of marketing and agency executives, called "The Future of Agency Relationships," researchers found that, over the past few years, the already-complex agency-marketer relationship has been significantly altered by factors such as the rise of social media. This has resulted in agencies quickly trying to expand their offerings, sometimes promising capabilities they are unable to deliver.

Sean Corcoran, an analyst at Forrester and lead author of
the report, said one of the biggest challenges marketers face
today is how to know who to turn to when they want to change
their ad strategies to include new media. He said it's further
complicated by the fact that the unbundled world of traditional,
PR, interactive, media, and direct agencies are trying to "bundle
themselves back up" to become jacks of all trades.

The Big Idea

The world of marketing is getting more complex. Today the
agency, the corporation, the retailer, and the consumer all have a
say in the brand's position.

Regardless of your lineup of agencies, as a marketer,
you are ultimately responsible for managing integrated
communications for your brand. If you abdicate that
responsibility, you run the risk of having your brand become
diluted. Even worse, just as Dove and Doritos brand managers
have learned the hard way, customers might come away with
entirely wrong perceptions about the meaning of your brand.
Let's not forget Geico and The Shane Company.

Outside of agency specialists, marketers are also dabbling with
how to incorporate social media into their marketing plans
themselves. Some have been experimenting with different types
of social media platforms for the past several years; others are
just now beginning to understand the true value that adding
social media to their overall promotional mix brings. Despite
an organization's experience with and tenure using social

media, marketers overwhelmingly are learning that social media programs are more effective when they are strategically integrated into the marketing mix than when they are used as standalone tactics.

INTEGRATING YOUR SOCIAL MEDIA CAMPAIGN

Anyone can create a Facebook or Twitter page. But what some have failed to recognize is that not only do those pages need to be maintained with relevant, worthwhile content, but they also need to meticulously mimic what the company is saying in all other media. Social media can't be considered just an add-on or an afterthought because others are using it. It has to be strategically integrated with all of your marketing communications, *even if that means starting fresh with a new approach.*

The most important issue is to establish a clear and consistent relationship between the social media you use and your traditional marketing efforts. A blog, for example, is a great way to get attention from your customers. When you have a potential customer's attention, it's time to funnel that person into your existing marketing model. Similarly, your Facebook page should contain the bare essentials of your marketing message and provide incentive for potential customers to visit your own Web site, walk through the doors of your business, or call and order a product. Driving fans to your Facebook page will do little for you if you can't then convert those fans into customers.

We've covered a lot of important topics in this chapter, so before we move on, let's take a quick look at the key concepts and action steps outlined on the previous pages.

▶ **Key concept:** Some brands have largely failed to integrate their communications campaigns with strong, long-lasting brand messages that resonate with customers over time, regardless of the touchpoint.

▶ **Action step:** Study the best practices of highly successful branding campaigns, such as those created for Chick-fil-A, Nike, and Apple.

▶ **Key concept:** Ultimately, your social media marketing strategies need to follow the same guiding principles as your other traditional marketing efforts.

▶ **Action step:** Keep your social media efforts narrowly focused on your target market, and try to use social media in a way that reflects your business's overall approach to integrated marketing communications.

▶ **Key concept:** Push-and-pull communications are here to stay. Marketers must align both forms in such a way that customers see the message as holistic, consistent, and originating from one source.

▶ **Action step:** Determine who will be responsible for managing marketing integration for your company and brand, and ensure that social media marketing efforts result in communications that are consistent with those of other vehicles.

WOULDN'T IT BE GREAT IF COKE HAD TO WORRY ABOUT ONLY PEPSI? OR IF HERTZ HAD TO WATCH OUT FOR ONLY AVIS? AND LIFE WOULD BE SIMPLE IF IBM WAS CONCERNED ONLY ABOUT APPLE. BUT THAT'S FAR FROM REALITY. IN MOST BUSINESSES, COMPETITION COMES NOT ONLY FROM YOUR DIRECT COMPETITORS, BUT ALSO FROM DIRECT, INDIRECT, INDUSTRY-SPECIFIC, AND GENERIC COMPETITORS.

CHAPTER 15

How to Conduct a
Competitive Assessment

As marketers develop their go-to-market strategies, they have to consider not only what their product or service has to offer, but also what their competitor's products or services have to offer.

The same principle applies when you think about your approach to an integrated social media campaign. It's important to start with a competitive assessment of your competitors' campaigns. Do they have a Facebook page? Are they Twitter aficionados? Do they blog like nobody's business? But it goes beyond that—you'll also want to analyze what they're doing *right*, what they might be doing *wrong*, and how you can do things differently to stand out.

CONDUCTING A COMPETITIVE ASSESSMENT FOR YOUR BUSINESS

Before we start talking about how a competitor's social media strategy can impact or influence your own, it's worth looking at how competition in business works. For example, book retailers such as Barnes & Noble and Borders have been facing the crunch of the recession and shifting demand resulting from new technologies. Just a few years ago, both retail brands were in head-to-head competition to see who could build the most megastores. While these massive bookstore chains were battling for physical retail dominance, an online empire called Amazon.com was being built with an almost unlimited selection of books. Today Barnes & Noble and Borders are playing catch-up to boost their own Web site traffic, in addition to managing their bricks-and-mortar locations.

The point is that competitive myopia, a focus on current competition and existing business models, can actually render a business extinct. For example, if Coke thinks that its only competition is Pepsi, then it's missing out on both opportunities and threats. Coke is most often consumed to satisfy thirst. However, other common reasons to drink a Coke include to feel revived or energized, to escape boredom, for a sugar fix, and for refreshment, along with a whole host of other reasons.

Who exactly competes with Coke in all of these areas? Take a look at the concentric circles in Figure 15.1. At the very basic level, Coke competes with other Cola brands such as Pepsi and RC Cola. At the next level of competition, Coke competes with other beverages, including water, juice, tea, and coffee, to quench thirst. At still another level, Coke competes at the level of providing satisfaction to the tired consumer, the bored consumer, or the consumer who just plain wants to drink something instead of eating.

Different Competitive Frames

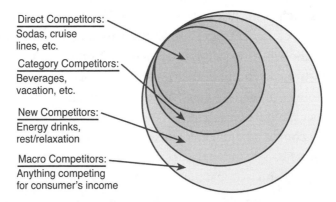

Direct Competitors:
Sodas, cruise lines, etc.

Category Competitors:
Beverages, vacation, etc.

New Competitors:
Energy drinks, rest/relaxation

Macro Competitors:
Anything competing for consumer's income

Figure 15.1 By understanding who your competitors are, you'll be better prepared to compete for consumers' disposable income.

At the broadest level, Coke competes with anything else that consumers could buy for the same amount of money they could spend on a Coke. Competition for dollars and the opportunity cost of using money to buy a Coke is the broadest form of competition. In this way, almost anything consumers would spend money on can be considered part of Coke's competitive set.

CONDUCTING A SOCIAL MEDIA COMPETITIVE ASSESSMENT

Another way to take a look at your competitive set is to create a simple two-dimensional mapping scheme that can help you compare your brand's attributes against your competitor's attributes (see Figure 15.2). For our purposes, this two-dimensional mapping scheme can compare your brand's social media campaigns against your competitor's social media campaigns.

On one axis, you might consider the number of different social media tools that companies use. On the other axis, you might consider the frequency with which social media is used to communicate. Of course, an infinite number of possible dimensions can be used for competitive mapping. The goal is to select the dimensions that make the most sense in the context of your business, your industry, and your set of competitors.

When you see where you are relative to your competition, you'll want to see how you can position yourself for success. Sure, many times a firm wants to place itself in exactly the same position as its closest competitor. Starbucks has

MyStarbucksIdea.com, so Caribou Coffee has to develop the exact same type of tool and hope for the same resulting success. If it worked for Starbucks, why wouldn't it work for Caribou? This strategy has some merits.

Other times you'll want to deliberately place yourself on the competitive grid as far away as possible from competitors. So if your nearest competitor has hired a specialist to manage its Facebook, Twitter, LinkedIn, and YouTube communications on a frequent basis, you might decide that you're interested in only a narrow set of tools—say, only blogs—and that you will contribute intermittently.

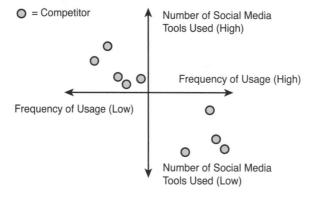

Figure 15.2 By plotting out how your competitors are using social media, you'll be able to analyze how to compete against them.

In reality, both of these approaches are at the extremes. To thwart competition, many clever companies deliberately segment, target, and position themselves to not directly compete. For example, when Southwest Airlines first came on the scene, management chose not to position the airline as just another airline. They were careful to consider the unique differentiators of Southwest's strategy—short flights, hub cities, relatively low prices, and hands-on service—to compare the Southwest travel experience to the alternative of driving, renting a car, taking a bus, or taking a train.

Similarly, when Walmart opened its first doors, it deliberately stayed away from the major metros where both Kmart and Sears dominated. Instead, it chose to locate its stores in rural areas and compete against smaller, independent retailers. When it dominated in that market, Walmart then had the muscle to penetrate urban locations and compete head to head against Kmart and Sears. The rest is history.

A final strategy that has worked well for some companies is to consider the concept of reverse positioning. Reverse positioning involves looking at what the major incumbents in your industry are doing, eliminating the obvious things that people offer in your business (sometimes doing the opposite), and adding several radically new points of difference.

As an example, Swedish furniture retailer IKEA uses reverse positioning. Most furniture stores provide high product quality, lots of product variety, lots of in-store assistance, and assembly and delivery. IKEA's positioning is average product quality, little variety within a category, little in-store assistance, and, until recently, no delivery and no assembly. How could they survive without the obvious "greens fees"? Instead of offering the obvious, they added a child care center, a sit-down restaurant featuring Swedish favorites, unique accessories with cool names and consistent, Scandinavian styling. The profit numbers show how successful this approach has been. Whereas most furniture store either have closed or are on the verge of bankruptcy, IKEAs store revenues have steadily increased over the past three decades.

The Big Idea

Some companies have found it better to zig while their competitors zag. This approach, called *reverse positioning*, has worked well for a variety of companies.

In the marketing communications space, smart marketers may want to replicate the IKEA success by including the competitive points of parity in terms of social media—must have a Web site, must have a Facebook page, must be using Twitter—and then think long and hard about what unique points of difference can successfully set it apart from the rest of its competitors. In terms of choice of social media tools, you want to analyze just how competition is using and benefiting from a specific tool and analyze whether it's worth the investment, given your marketing objectives.

A final point of comparison with marketing communications campaigns is their timing and intensity relative to competitive messages. Most traditional media have periods of "on" and "off" in terms of media scheduling. It's important for you to know when competitors have planned your communications and around what events as you plan for your own. With new media, particularly with pull-based social media, the conversation is ongoing. You have a lesser need to plan and time your actions based on your competition—and the same holds for them. So the only thing left is to make sure that your communications are consistent with your desired brand positioning and that your social media communications are integrated with the rest of your communications portfolio.

Let's take a look at the key concepts and action steps from this chapter.

- ▶ **Key concept:** You can analyze your competitive environment based on direct competitors, category competitors, new competitors, and macro competitors.

- ▶ **Action step:** Don't get myopic when thinking about your competition. In the broadest sense, every brand competes against every other brand for consumers' finite amount of disposable income.

- ▶ **Key concept:** By analyzing how your competitors are using social media, you can get a sense of what's working and what's not working within your industry.

- ▶ **Action step:** Analyze how your competitors are using social media to grow their business. Do a quick cost/benefit analysis to figure out what would work for your business and what wouldn't work.

- ▶ **Key concept:** Identifying how your competitors impact your business is critical to developing your unique positioning within the social media space.

- ▶ **Action step:** Try your hand at reverse positioning—remember IKEA versus all those now-defunct furniture companies—by monitoring the tools your competitors are using in the social media space. Either move away from them altogether or augment them with entirely unique tools or creative ways to use the tools.

EVERY GOOD MARKETING PLAN STARTS WITH A *SITUATION ANALYSIS*. IT'S THE FOUNDATION UPON WHICH A COMPANY'S MARKETING GOALS, OBJECTIVES, STRATEGIES, AND TACTICS ARE BUILT.

CHAPTER 16

CONDUCTING AN INTERNAL
SITUATION ANALYSIS

When an organization develops a strategic plan of any kind, it must consider a number of things. It needs to consider the external environments in which it operates. It must fully understand the competitive landscape and where possible opportunity gaps exist. It has to develop a strong understanding of its prospects and customers to create a value proposition that resonates. Finally, it has to do an *internal situation analysis* to leverage strengths and downplay weaknesses.

This last factor, an internal situation analysis, is an important one. It's often overlooked because companies tend to shy away from doing a 360-degree analysis of their own strengths and weaknesses. Don't make that mistake. The only way you can know how to move forward with a successful social media campaign is to take a long, hard look at the "internal situation analysis mirror."

The Big Idea

A situation analysis can help you analyze what's working and what's not working within your current marketing program. Before you move forward with your social media campaign, take a step back and do a situation analysis first.

CONDUCTING AN INTERNAL SITUATION ANALYSIS

In a typical marketing planning process, an internal organizational analysis looks at the relevant areas involving the product/service offering and the organization itself. In the same way, when you're thinking about social media planning, you need to review the successes and failures of past programs. In doing so, you will need to consider the fit between your desired social media strategy and the way your company is currently structured and operates.

You also need to look at the relative advantages and disadvantages of conducting social media activities in-house, as opposed to hiring an external agency or agencies. For example, the internal analysis may indicate that a firm is not capable of planning, implementing, and managing certain areas of the social media program. In this case, it might be wise to look for outside help in the form of a specialized agency.

Before you decide on hiring an outside agency, you have to consider whether outsourcing a specific communications function will result in a loss of control or speed, and whether the resulting benefits of expertise and time will outweigh the negatives. For instance, both Calvin Klein and Macy's develop all their communications in-house. Macy's chooses to stay in-house because of the high frequency of communications and the need to stay on top of constant changes. Calvin Klein keeps communications in-house to retain complete control over the creative message and the brand's positioning.

In contrast, both Anheuser-Busch and Frito-Lay have traditionally chosen to work with large integrated marketing communications firms. Their belief is that specialized agencies will add more expertise to the communications process and will be able to develop creative marketing materials and content unique to each brand's position. After all, marketing communications firms are the experts when it comes to communications. Recently, however, Frito-Lay has deviated from its typical model of outsourcing to an agency model by allowing user-generated advertising content for its Doritos brand. This may save Frito-Lay significant money, because the company doesn't have to pay for the agency's work, but it also risks altering the brand message because neither internal nor external "experts" are working on developing the brand communications.

CONDUCTING A SWOT ANALYSIS

An internal situational analysis also assesses the relative strengths, weaknesses, opportunities, and threats (SWOT) of the product or service you're trying to sell. This information is particularly important to the creative personnel who must develop the communications message for the brand or company. Completing a SWOT analysis helps you identify ways to minimize the effect of weaknesses in your business while maximizing your strengths. Ideally, you'll match your strengths against market opportunities that result from your competitors' weaknesses or voids.

Here are some considerations when you do your social media SWOT analysis:

- ▶ **Strengths**—Think about what your company does well in terms of social media marketing. What makes you stand out from your competitors, and what they are doing? What advantages do you have over other businesses?

▶ **Weaknesses**—Identify what areas are a struggle from a management perspective? What resource limitations exist from a personnel perspective? What time constraints are present?

▶ **Opportunities**—Try to uncover areas where your strengths are not being fully utilized. Are there emerging trends that fit with your company's strengths?

▶ **Threats**—Look both inside and outside your company for factors that could damage your business. Internally, do you have financial, development, or other problems? Externally, are your competitors becoming stronger through either their expertise or their messaging? Are emerging trends amplifying one of your weaknesses, or do you see other threats to your organization's success?

An internal situation analysis also involves assessing the strengths and weaknesses of the organization from an *image* perspective. The image an organization brings to the market has a significant impact on the way it can advertise and promote itself along with its various products and services. Companies or brands that are new to the market or those whose perceptions are negative may have to concentrate on their images, not just on the attributes and benefits of the products they sell. On the other hand, an organization with a strong reputation is already a step ahead when it comes to communication about its products or services.

For example, a recent nationwide survey found that companies with the best overall reputations among American consumers are Johnson & Johnson, The Coca-Cola Company, Hewlett-Packard,

Intel, and Ben & Jerry's. When an organization's leaders understand what's at the core of their positive image, they can use it to grow their business. For example, Ben & Jerry's is regarded as a good citizen in its dealings with communities, employees, and the environment. The company capitalizes on this goodwill by supporting various community events and participating in programs that help the environment. That's good news for the nonprofits that benefit from Ben & Jerry's kindness, and it's good news for the Ben & Jerry's consumers, who know that a portion of each purchase goes to benefit those in need.

Did You Know?

The Ben & Jerry's Foundation donates almost $2 million each year to worthy causes around the U.S. This helps the nonprofits run their programs and also helps create a positive impression among Ben & Jerry's consumers.[1]

HOW TO MOVE AHEAD

For most organizations, developing a social media strategy involves some fundamental questions: How do the benefits of engaging in social media outweigh the risks? How can social media influence key organizational stakeholders in a way that benefits the organization? Does the organization have the capabilities needed to achieve its desired positioning by including social media in the communications mix?

Let's look at each of these questions in more detail. When people talk about benefits and risks, they usually think about the benefits and risks of engaging in a certain action. Often overlooked are the risks of *not* engaging in a certain action. For example, if company is sitting on the social media sidelines, the inaction is creating a vacuum that's being filled by comments, blog posts, and tweets circulating on the Web. That can be a dangerous situation.

So if it doesn't pay to sit on the sidelines, why do some companies do just that? According to a 2009 Marketing Sherpa survey of senior-level marketing managers, the most significant barrier to social media adoption named by 46 percent of respondents is "lack of knowledgeable staff" (see Figure 16.1). The problem is, a good percentage of those who consider themselves knowledgeable have limited social media experience. In fact, two-thirds of marketers at organizations that have not used social media marketing said they are "very" or "somewhat" knowledgeable about the subject. But without hands-on social media experience, this level of knowledge isn't very likely. It may be the reason "lack of knowledgeable staff" is seen as the most significant barrier.

What does all this mean? In a nutshell, it points out that, before you can move forward, it's best to take a step back. When you take a step back and conduct a situation analysis, you'll be able to get a clear picture of the strengths, weaknesses, opportunities, and threats facing your company. Only then will you be prepared to move forward to the next steps of looking at the consumer thought process, clarifying objectives, and developing key strategies designed to help you achieve those objectives.

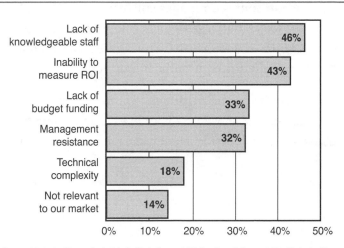

Source: MarketingSherpa Social Media Marketing and PR Benchmark Survey 2008. MarketingSherpa © 2009.
Methodology: Fielded December 4-10, 2008; N=1,886.

Figure 16.1   What factors have prevented you from having a successful
social media campaign?

Let's review these key concepts and action steps before moving
on to the next chapter.

▶ **Key concept:** A critical component in developing your
social media strategy and plan is understanding your
organization's internal situation and determining whether
you have the right structure, resources, and capabilities to
manage social media in-house.

▶ **Action step:** Perform a SWOT analysis of your organization
in terms of your ability to set up, run, and manage a social
media campaign.

▶ **Key concept:** Some companies still fear moving ahead with their social media strategy development because they lack the knowledge of how to incorporate social media into their marketing communications plans.

▶ **Action step:** If you feel as though running a social media campaign in-house will take your eye off of running your business, hire an outside agency to develop it and run it for you.

ENDNOTES

1. See BenAndJerrysFoundation.org.

THE GOAL OF MARKETING IS TO "GET MORE PEOPLE TO BUY MORE OF YOUR STUFF, MORE OFTEN, FOR MORE MONEY MORE EFFICIENTLY AND EFFECTIVELY THAN THEY BUY YOUR COMPETITOR'S STUFF."

CHAPTER 17

UNDERSTANDING THE CUSTOMER THOUGHT PROCESSES

This phrase, describing the objectives for any marketer, comes from Sergio Zyman, the first chief marketing officer of The Coca-Cola Company. It sounds simple enough. In reality, doing all the activities in this short phrase requires disciplined strategy, focused operational detail, and a well-oiled organizational machine. Most importantly, it requires a complete understanding of the needs of your customers so that you can "get more people to buy your stuff" over and over again. Often this is the hardest thing for an organization to do. It has to get inside the heads of its customers and prospective customers to understand what they truly want.

Having a strong understanding of what customers need involves being able to get an accurate picture of what they *think* they need. It also involves figuring out what they might need even if they don't tell you explicitly. That's the hard part.

To do this, you need to understand how customers make decisions and then understand how they respond to various stimuli, whether it's a traditional ad campaign or a social media campaign.

CUSTOMER DECISION-MAKING PROCESS

We've discussed a variety of customer decision-making models in previous chapters. They all point out that the decision-making process typically begins when a gap exists between the actual state people are in and their desired state (see Figure 17.1). This first stage, the problem recognition stage, occurs when a customer perceives a need and becomes motivated to solve the problem, as in, "I have a headache. I'd like to *not* have a headache."

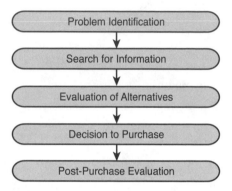

Figure 17.1 Consumers move through a series of states before, during, and after purchase.

For the most part, customers recognize that they have a need on their own. However, sometimes a marketer may be able to influence problem recognition by encouraging customers to be discontent with their current state or situation. For example, communications about personal hygiene products such as mouthwash, deodorant, and foot sprays may be designed to create insecurities that people can resolve by using these products.

The next stage in the process involves searching for information needed to make a purchase decision. Typically, this stage involves a prospect or customer's memories about past experiences with the brand. That is, if a search within one's own memory or past experiences does not result in enough information, the customer will seek additional information by searching for it in ads, on the Web, on television, or through some other medium. During this stage, a marketer can influence the decision through advertising, salespeople, point-of-purchase displays and online tools. The main goal for a marketer is to attempt to get a particular product into the customer's considered set of alternatives.

After getting information during the information search stage, a customer starts looking at alternatives. During this stage, the customer compares the various products and brands under consideration that are likely to help solve the initial problem. To tip a customer toward one alternative over another, the marketer needs to help the customer form positive attitude towards a certain brand or get the customer to change a negative attitude into a positive one.

The fourth stage in decision making is the actual purchase decision itself. After a customer has evaluated alternatives, that customer may develop a purchase intention or predisposition to buy a certain brand. However, a purchase decision is not the same as an actual purchase. The customer must still *make* the purchase. She still has to decide where to purchase, when to purchase, how much to spend, and so on. Considerable amounts of time can lapse between the *decision* to purchase and the *actual* purchase, particularly for high-involvement (such as high-dollar) purchases. As a result, almost half the time, a customer who has decided to purchase Brand A actually ends up buying Brand B.

Did You Know?

Research indicates that 47 percent of the time, a customer will report wanting to buy one product and end up buying a different product instead.[1]

Why is all this important? Because whether you're developing a social media campaign or a traditional marketing campaign, it's important to understand *how* and *why* people buy products. By gaining insights into consumer behavior, you can improve the effectiveness of your campaign by taking actual consumer insights into consideration—and, in the long run, make more money.

DECISION MAKING WHEN IT REALLY MATTERS

Let's consider a high-involvement decision: selecting which college to attend. This comes down to finding the right "fit." Students must determine which college lines up with their values, interests, and personality, and evaluate the university's academic programs, reputation, student life, cost, and other factors. In the end, prospective students must "feel right" about the college they choose.

Here's where social media comes in. How prospective students gather information to find that "good fit" has changed dramatically in the past 20 years. In those days, information and advice came from a narrow range of experts: school guidance counselors and whatever catalogs and directories happened to be on hand at the resource center. A few books on college admissions were written, but not many. No national rankings existed yet. Conversations with peers and perhaps other friends and family members were important, and noting where those others were going or had gone to college had an impact. But overall, the people who had an impact on this choice came from within a small, geographically defined circle.

The Big Idea

Most decisions to buy a product happen after some experience or engagement with a brand. Social media can impact customers at various points in their decision-making process, thereby improving the ROI of your overall marketing campaign.

Since then, of course, the availability of information has grown tremendously in the form of direct marketing, glossy brochures, national rankings, published guidebooks, paid consultants and seminars, and even classes for high schoolers. Add to this the vast amounts of information available online from a variety of sources, including colleges themselves. Just the information to guide the "fit" decision is truly overwhelming, and sorting through it is as big a challenge as making the eventual decision.

Now add social media to the mix. The question is whether it will add value, by providing new kinds of information or by making it easier to sift through the most useful, relevant information from the marketplace of sources. One attribute that clearly distinguishes social media from other sources is that it makes peers more immediately and dynamically available. Prospective students are no longer limited to conversations with students at their own school or to the few students and alumni they encounter on a college tour or a campus event. They're not even limited by the representative peers quoted in a guidebook. Using social media, they can largely bypass college officials, consultants, and other "experts"—not to mention parents— and connect with peers from the national and even global landscape.

How will these connections made possible by social media, in conjunction with traditional media, influence the decisions of prospects and the admissions and marketing strategies of colleges and universities? Will the marketing efforts of colleges and all those "adult" voices and experts become less influential now that prospects can access the "authentic voice," or at least voices that feel authentic because they come from peers?

Prospective students find social media conversations attractive and useful because the voices are authentic and impartial. Information has already been democratized; schools such as MIT that present student blogs on their admissions Web sites are acknowledging the situation—and perhaps trying to create a competitive advantage by bringing some of those conversations "in-house." As the volume of choice and information grows, consumers turn to the sources they feel they can trust.

Did You Know?

Seventy percent of the respondents to a survey by Nielsen "completely" trusted or "somewhat" trusted recommendations from consumer opinions posted online. That was second only to "recommendations from people known," which came in at 90 percent.[2]

The customer decision process doesn't end with a purchase. After using the product or service, a customer compares the level of performance with expectations and is either satisfied or dissatisfied. Positive performance means that the brand stays in a customer's evoked set of brands, and there's a strong likelihood that the customer will choose the brand chosen again. A negative performance may lead the customer to form negative attitudes toward the brand, decreasing the likelihood that the customer will purchase the brand again, or even causing it to drop out of the customer's evoked set.

THE ROLE OF SOCIAL MEDIA IN INFLUENCING DECISIONS

So how does social media tie into the customer's decision-making process? At first glance, it may seem that the main purpose of social media is to drive awareness and to perhaps impact the problem recognition stage. After all, more people are having conversations about a company, a product, or a brand before the actual purchase. However, the real value of social media might lie in the consideration stage, or the alternative evaluation stage, in terms of establishing relevance. Customers are more likely to consider a product or service that their friends or other people like them have recommended than they are to consider one recommended by outside sources that they don't know. Social media therefore helps customers reduce their choice by narrowing the list to a smaller set of possible alternatives.

Moreover, marketers must recognize the importance of the post-purchase evaluation stage of decision making. Dissatisfied customers who experience post-purchase doubt or have had a negative experience not only are unlikely to rebuy, but also may spread negative word-of-mouth information that deters others from purchasing a particular product or service. In this way, blogs, consumer ratings, and product reviews can directly impact future customer decision making and choice.

In addition to understanding the complexities of customer decision making, you must understand consumer response to communications. Consumer response refers to the various steps or processes that those who receive communications may go through in moving toward a specific behavior (such as purchasing a product) and how the promotional efforts of a marketer influence consumer response.

Many models of consumer response have been developed, but one of the most relevant models to the inclusion of social media in the communications mix is the AIDA model (see Figure 17.2). We mentioned AIDA in Chapter 4, "The Language of Social Media," but let's briefly recap what it's all about. AIDA stands for Awareness, Interest, Desire, and Action. The model was first developed to represent the stages through which a salesperson must take a customer in the personal selling process. First, a marketing campaign (or sales person) must get the customer's *attention*. Then it must arouse some *interest* in the product or service. Strong levels of interest should create a *desire* to own or use the product. Finally, the *action* stage involves getting the customer to make a purchase commitment and closing the sale.

Consumer Behavior Models

	AIDA Model	Hierarchy of Effects Model	Innovation Adoption Model	Information Processing Model
Cognition Phase	Attention	Awareness, Knowledge	Awareness	Presentation, Attention, Comprehension
Affective Phase	Interest, Desire	Liking, Preference, Conviction	Interest, Evaluation	Yielding, Retention
Behavioral Phase	Action	Purchase	Adoption	Behavior

Figure 17.2   A variety of different consumer behavior models exist, but they all point to the same goal: converting a prospect to a customer.

Different forms of communication have been shown to have varying effects on the response stages. Advertising is largely effective in driving awareness. Direct mail and Web sites are strong drivers of interest. Personal selling and PR are often responsible for driving desire, and sales promotion often leads to action by encouraging trial. The impact of these different media types varies depending on the level of involvement a customer has with the product category and based on the degree of differentiation between alternatives.

As with traditional media, social media also can be segmented to reflect what consumer response it can best achieve. So far, this has not been done in any formal way. Perhaps Twitter is the strongest tool for driving awareness. LinkedIn might be best for driving interest. Facebook is likely to help develop desire. In terms of action, search engine optimization (SEO) and direct response marketing may be the strongest drivers. Still left to be determined is exactly what messages work best with which form of social media and whether the tools can evolve through technology to achieve multiple customer responses at varying places in the response process.

With all this in mind, let's take a spin through the key concepts and action steps from this chapter:

▶ **Key concept:** Customers follow a consistent process when they are making decisions. Marketers can influence the sequence of these stages and how long a customer takes in each of these decision stages.

▶ **Action step:** Map out the decision-making process for different segments of customers, and understand where and how you can influence this decision making with a variety of social media tools

▶ **Key concept:** Customers follow specific patterns of response based on their exposure to marketing stimuli, their level of involvement in the product, and the degree of differentiation they perceive among competing alternatives.

▶ **Action step:** Understand the level of involvement your customer has with your product or brand, and determine how differentiated you are from your competitors. These two factors will impact the actual response pattern customers follow and will help you determine which social media stimuli to use.

ENDNOTES

1. J. Scott Armstrong, Vicki G. Morwitz, and V. Kumar, "Sales Forecasts for Existing Consumer Products and Services: Do Purchase Intentions Contribute to Accuracy?" *International Journal of Forecasting* 16 (2000): 383–397.

2. http://blog.nielsen.com/nielsenwire/consumer/global-advertising-consumers-trust-real-friends-and-virtual-strangers-the-most/

THE DETROIT ZOO HAD
BEEN AN INSTITUTION AND
A TOURIST DESTINATION
FOR MORE THAN 80
YEARS, BUT IT NOW HAD A
PROBLEM. UNBEKNOWNST
TO MOST VISITORS,
IT FACED FINANCIAL
HARDSHIP CAUSED BY
CIRCUMSTANCES THAT
HAD BEGUN A FEW YEARS
EARLIER.

CHAPTER 18

Establishing Your Major Objectives and Key Strategies

The city of Detroit, which provided a significant portion of the zoo's operating budget, cut all of its financial support of zoo operations in 2006. As the 2008 peak summer season approached, reality set in: In a matter of months, the money would run out. The zoo was faced with the very real possibility of closing its doors.

Only one option was left. The zoo had to appeal directly to taxpayers. A new tax was proposed to provide the necessary funding to keep the zoo afloat. Zoo management had to convince voters to pass the requested new tax, or the zoo would close. With the very real possibility that there would no longer be a Detroit Zoo and the impact that would have on the children of Detroit, zoo officials had just one objective for an integrated marketing campaign they were planning to launch: Get residents to vote "yes" on a new ten-year property tax to support the zoo.

Zoo management could have simply created an awareness campaign highlighting all the great attractions at the zoo. Or it could have created a promotional campaign appealing to visitors by offering some sort of discount or incentive. Instead, it chose to stay focused on the main issue at hand: raising money to keep the zoo afloat. By taking a step back and thinking through the situation before taking a step forward, they were able to identify three important factors leading to a successful campaign: the key drivers, the primary objectives, and the desired outcomes.

DON'T JUST CREATE AN ACTION— CREATE A CHAIN REACTION

Zoo management knew that it needed a message that would provoke not just action, but a chain reaction. They distilled the big idea into a single concept: *Our Zoo Is Worth Keeping*. They also made it personal—"The Detroit Zoo Is *Our* Zoo"—and highly emotional, drawing attention to the interaction children have with the animals at the Zoo. By tapping into these key emotional drivers, they were able to set themselves up for success.

Advertising led this initiative, but it involved more than just a traditional advertising message. It relied on a powerful dialogue that used mass media and new media to create a conversation in the news and on the streets. A public relations and grass roots effort to get the "Worth Keeping" message to both residents and influencers kept the conversation front and center in the news for about a month leading up to the election.

When the vote was finally taken, zoo officials were pleased to find that voters had approved the new tax with larger margins than anyone had imagined. Having achieved this, zoo management was in a position to implement some of the strategies required to get people not only to see the zoo in a new light, but also to become re-engaged with the zoo in terms of attendance, volunteering, and finances.

HOW TO SET OBJECTIVES THAT GET YOU RESULTS

The main point of the Detroit Zoo example is that results such as these are attainable only when you 1) identify the *key drivers* for success, 2) develop specific *campaign objectives,* and 3) know exactly which *outcomes* you are seeking to achieve. The trick is to think through all this first, before you start to develop your approach or your strategy to achieve them.

Setting objectives and developing strategy takes discipline. It takes forming a unified view of the problem, making an assessment about desired outcomes, and having a shared vision within your organization on how to achieve those outcomes.

If you're thinking that your organization has had trouble articulating just what you hope to achieve by using social media, you're not alone. Unfortunately, many organizations have difficulty when it comes to setting realistic objectives for a social media program.

The Big Idea

When setting social media objectives, it's important to be SMART. In other words, you need to set objectives that are specific, measurable, attainable, realistic, and time bound. Only then can you **determine the best strategy** to take and the best customers to target.

Numerous articles and blog posts talk about how to set
objectives for a social media campaign. The objectives
mentioned range from driving Web site traffic to increasing
customer engagement. But no matter what your stated
objectives are, only one thing is important: You need to
integrate your social media campaign into your marketing
campaign so that they can both show a quantifiable return on
your investment.

MOVING PRODUCT

To many managers, the only meaningful objective for their
promotional strategies is sales. They take the position that the
basic reason to spend money on any kind of communications,
including communications via social media, is to sell a product
or service. This makes a lot of sense. Ultimately, the goal of
any marketing program is to sell more products or services,
resulting in more revenue, higher market share, and more
profit.

Recently, two of the three largest oral care manufacturers,
Unilever and Colgate–Palmolive, joined Procter & Gamble
in marketing at-home tooth-whitening kits. In their product
launches, Unilever spent about $20 million on Mentadent
and Colgate allocated $60 million to Simply White. Colgate's
objective was to get an immediate $100 million in sales in the
first year (a third of the total market); Mentadent focused on
in-store efforts, sales promotions, ads in beauty magazines and

on their Web sites, and professional outreach programs to gain its share of the market.

Sales-oriented objectives such as the ones Unilever and Colgate–Palmolive set for themselves can make a great deal of sense. But focusing only on sales objectives has its challenges. In the real world, poor sales can result from a number of uncontrollable factors, including product design, quality, packaging, distribution, pricing, demographic trends, and competitor actions. Furthermore, social media can make people aware of a brand, but it can't make them buy it—particularly if something else is fundamentally wrong. For example, in the early 1990s, when Nabisco launched Snackwells, a line of reduced-fat and nonfat cookies, the advertising for Snackwells is what drove consumers to the stores. The advertising was brilliant, but the factories couldn't meet the rate of the demand and the store shelves were always short of packages.

Another problem with considering only sales-oriented objectives for social media is that the effects of advertising often occur over an extended period of time. Your social media marketing efforts can have a lag or a carryover effect. In other words, the money and time that you spend on social media efforts don't necessarily have an immediate effect on sales. That doesn't mean you should abandon your efforts. If you're trying to grow your sales, you need to consider that the impact of social media may emerge over time and that, besides sales, social media may help you achieve other important milestones that lead to revenue growth.

Did You Know?

During the 2.7 hours per day that people in the U.S. spend on the mobile Web, 45 percent are posting comments on social networks, 43 percent are connecting with friends on social networks, 40 percent are sharing content with others, and 38 percent are sharing photos.[1]

MOVING PEOPLE

As we described in early sections of the book, marketing communications can have a cumulative effect over time and can result in various intermediate stages of persuasion that eventually lead to sales. Advertising and other forms of promotion, including all forms of social media, are designed to achieve communications such as brand knowledge and interest, favorable attitudes and image, and purchase intentions or leads. With some types of communication, you can't expect a direct sales response immediately. Instead, marketers realize that they have to provide relevant information and create favorable predispositions toward a brand before customers purchase anything.

The Communications Effect Pyramid (see Figure 18.1) depicts the way social media helps move people—or trigger some kind of presales response. At the lower level of the pyramid, your brand's communications first get people to pay attention to and become knowledgeable about the product or service. At the next level, the goal is to get people to develop an interest, a liking, and perhaps even a preference for your product or service. Beyond knowledge, you want people to develop feelings. Finally, at the top of the pyramid comes action. At this top level, people develop strong convictions, form purchase intentions, and finally purchase.

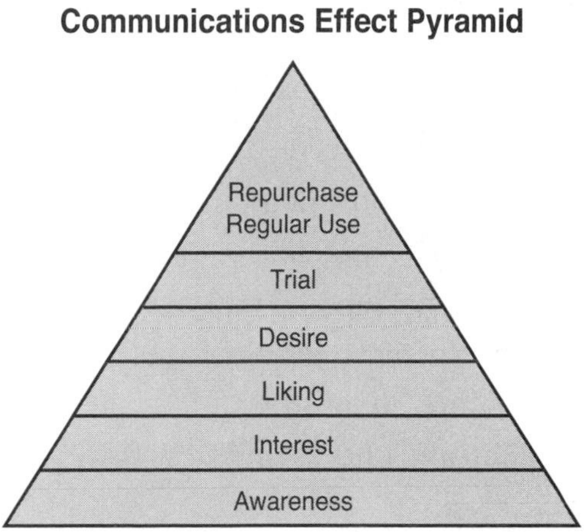

Communications Effect Pyramid

Figure 18.1 Understanding the consumer response process is one step involved in setting objectives for your campaign.

Part of driving communications objectives involves encouraging prospective customers to start dialogues with you and with each other about your products and services. You want to get them engaged so that, over time, you can convert them to customers. If you do this correctly, existing customers will not only repurchase from you, but they will become strong advocates for your brand and help you continue the dialogue within and outside your brand community.

Whether you decide to focus on using your social media to drive immediate sales or future sales often depends upon where you sit in an organization. If you're in the CEO or CFO office, you may be interested in driving immediate sales so that this quarter's numbers look good to Wall Street. But if you're in the CMO office or on the agency side, you might believe that building long-term demand is just as important as generating short-term sales blips.

In the end, the path you choose might boil down to whether you consider your social marketing efforts to be an investment that will show returns at some point in the future or whether you consider your social marketing efforts to be an investment that you must quickly recoup. To know how to balance these two major objectives of moving product and moving people, you might have to think about who is sitting in the CEO seat of your organization and understand what drives that person's business strategy.

DEVELOPING YOUR SOCIAL MEDIA STRATEGY

After you've outlined your specific social media objectives, you're ready to develop a social media strategy. Your social media strategy is a subset of your overall marketing strategy. And your marketing strategy is a subset of your business strategy.

Keep all these factors in mind as you move forward with a social media campaign. After all, one-off marketing campaigns that create short-term blips don't grow a business in the long run.

Only well-thought-out campaigns with an eye toward strategy and execution succeed.

A successful social media campaign isn't something to merely play around with in between meetings or to give to an intern as a task to complete over the summer. It should be an intentional, thought-provoking extension of your organization that helps you drive your business objectives.

Companies often ask themselves these questions when developing an overall business strategy:

- ▶ Should we be first to market and enjoy first mover advantages, or should we pursue a wait-and-follow approach?

- ▶ Should we try to enter with a low cost position, or should we try to distinguish ourselves from competitors with a differentiated offering?

- ▶ Should we approach the market as a whole, or should we focus on a single or a few niche segments?

- ▶ Should we grow our business by encouraging more sales of our existing product to our existing customers, by introducing new products, by entering new markets, or all three?

Take a look at these questions and develop answers for your own company. Then take a step back and analyze whether the social media strategy you're developing fits within the business strategy you've outlined from similar questions. You'll then have taken the first steps toward developing a methodical, strategic approach to a successful social media campaign.

We've covered a lot of ground again. Let's take a quick look at the key concepts from this chapter and their action steps.

▶ **Key concept:** When developing any marketing campaign, you need to 1) identify the *key drivers* for success, 2) develop specific *campaign objectives*, and 3) know exactly which *outcomes* you are seeking to achieve.

▶ **Action step:** Get all members of your marketing team in a room together (along with other interested parties) and map out key drivers, campaign objectives, and outcomes for your social media campaign.

▶ **Key concept:** Social media objectives can be categorized into two major buckets. The first objective is to move product to drive *immediate* sales. The second objective is to move people (that is, drive awareness, interest, and desire) to drive *future* sales.

▶ **Action step:** Find out what your organization expects in terms of return on investment and the time frame for that return. You can then determine whether your social media campaign needs to drive immediate sales or future sales. Remember, they're not mutually exclusive—if you have a big budget, you can accomplish both.

▶ **Key concept:** When using social media, it's critical for your campaign to tie to your business objectives and for these business objectives to link to your overall business strategy.

▶ **Action step:** Make sure you clearly understand your organization's business objectives and the strategy it's using to accomplish those objectives. Ask key players within your organization to define the business objectives and strategy or to direct you to the appropriate documentation.

ENDNOTES

1. See www.readwriteweb.com/archives/social_networking_now_more_popular_on_mobile_than_desktop.php.

ONE OF THE BIGGEST
MISTAKES PEOPLE MAKE
WHEN SETTING UP A
SOCIAL MEDIA CAMPAIGN
IS TO NOT ALIGN THEIR
SOCIAL MEDIA CAMPAIGN
WITH THEIR PRIMARY
MARKETING CAMPAIGN. AS
A RESULT, THEY TALK TO
CONSUMERS WITH TWO
DIFFERENT VOICES, WHICH
IS NEVER A GOOD IDEA.

CHAPTER 19

ALIGNING YOUR SOCIAL MEDIA
STRATEGY WITH YOUR BRAND
ESSENCE

In this chapter, we talk about aligning your social media campaign with your brand. What is a brand? A brand is often defined as the sum total of consumer's perceptions and feelings about the product attributes, how they perform, and the benefits they provide to the consumer. Said another way, a brand is both the spoken and unspoken messages a consumer receives about your product or service.

Brands are created through a wide range of touchpoints. Every time a customer interacts with your brand, the customer forms associations. In this way, a brand is much like the promise of a specific customer experience.

The Big Idea

Articulating your brand essence through your social media strategy is the key to successful marketing. Whatever you want your brand to represent should be articulated and demonstrated in your social media communication efforts.

The most successful brands have established a relevant, differentiated meaning for themselves and have reduced this meaningful difference to a simple, clear, and cohesive thought. This clear and concise articulation of what a brand stands for is known as *brand essence.*

Does all that make sense? Sometimes brand theory and brand strategy can get a little over-the-top, but the bottom line is that a brand is the sum total of the experiences and perceptions a prospect or customer has about your product or service.

THE ESSENCE OF BRAND ESSENCE

Think of brand essence as the heart and soul of a product or service. It represents the relationship your brand has with your customer. For example, Hallmark uses the phrase, "Enriching Lives" to capture its brand essence and its company culture. "Enriching Lives" represents the basis for how Hallmark serves customers, develops its products, communicates its marketing messages, develops merchandising for its stores, and creates a positive work environment for employees. Hallmark's brand essence permeates every aspect of the company and business, and it has continued to serve the brand over time.

Similarly, Harley-Davidson's brand essence has created a fiercely loyal customer base that connects to the brand emotionally. Harley-Davidson's image doesn't simply reflect the quality and design of its motorcycles. Rather, the brand is best known for the value it places on nonconformity and self-determination. That's why buyers believe that owning a Harley makes a powerful, strong statement to others that they live life on their own terms.

Did You Know?

If you want to get a basic understanding of your brand essence, you can do three simple things:

1. Conduct external focus groups or surveys with customers and prospects to uncover their impressions of your brand.

2. Conduct internal focus groups or surveys with your employees to uncover their impressions of your brand.

3. Compare and contrast your findings to begin to understand
the current *essence* of your brand.

Getting a deep understanding of your brand essence is often
much more complicated than what we've outlined here, but if
you want a basic understanding, you can follow these three
simple steps.

Before you begin thinking about how to align your social media
efforts with your brand, you must first articulate exactly what
your brand stands for or means. You also need to know how your
prospects, customers, and employees interpret that meaning.
For example, when you think about the brand Volvo, the word
safety immediately comes to mind. In contrast, when you think
about the brand Rolls Royce, *luxury* comes to mind. Of course,
there are elements of safety within the Rolls Royce brand and
elements of luxury in some models of Volvo, but the primary
promise of each of these brands forms its unique essence.

It may sound simple to articulate your brand's meaning or
essence, but this can be a challenging endeavor. Several gaps
may exist. First, there could be gap between your existing brand
articulation and what you would like your brand to represent.
For example, Mercedes may want to retain its positioning as
a luxury brand, but that's not the current perception people
have of the brand as it has rolled out several lower priced line
extensions during the last decade or so. Another gap may be
between your intended brand positioning and the actions
you take to communicate that positioning. Going back to the
Mercedes example, Mercedes may want to exemplify luxury, but
rolling out a line of cars priced under $30,000, a line of bicycles,

and even children's tricycles goes against a luxury positioning. That's a disconnect from the consumer's point of view.

ALIGNING YOUR EFFORTS WITH YOUR BRAND

When you have a good handle on your brand's essence, you need to think about how to communicate that essence through traditional and new media. This is where social media comes in. With the right content on your blog posts, tweets, and Facebook Fan Pages, you have the potential to spread your brand messages quickly across a wide range of audiences. However, you must ensure that the content you develop is consistent with the image you want to portray. Putting out quality and focused content helps you establish your brand only if your content supports your brand's essence and positioning.

The goal of social media is to help you develop personal relationships between your brand and your target audience. The interactive aspect of social media is personal by nature, so the relationships you create can be *deeper and longer lasting* than with any other media. To maintain those relationships, make sure your brand comes across as authentic and transparent. One of the keys is to be consistent in what you say and do in your social media campaign.

Let's take a look at an example of a misaligned social media campaign and then consider an example of a well-aligned social media campaign, to put what we've articulated into context.

THE GOOD, THE BAD, AND THE UGLY

In 2009, when Honda decided to publish its soon-to-launch Crosstour's photos on Facebook, it should have been ready for some serious feedback. Within a short time, its fan page was flooded with negative comments regarding the look of Honda's new Cross Utility Vehicle. Most "fans" clearly were not too thrilled with the new design. But soon afterward, they saw some positive comments about the model. The problem was, the positive comments were coming from Honda's product manager, who didn't disclose his own relationship with the company until the angry fans called him out. This likely made people think twice about Honda's ability to be true to its brand essence.

Did You Know?

A negative remark on social media equates to a loss of 30 potential customers—but this also means that a positive review may help you gain 30 new customers.[1]

Of course, companies need to use social media to promote their products, but if they get bad feedback, they shouldn't try to manipulate it. Social media users are savvy enough to expose you if they want to. Honesty and authenticity are critical to success in this space.

In contrast to the Honda example, let's take a look at a company that seems to have done everything right to align its social media strategy with its brand and what it stands for. Everyone talks about using social media to connect with customers and engage in deeper relationships and conversations, but few companies are able to do it well. One company that seems to be doing this right is Starbucks.

The Starbucks strategy involves several elements, including a presence on Facebook, Twitter, YouTube, and Flickr. As mentioned previously, one of the company's key social media tactics has been to develop the MyStarbucksIdea.com Web site. My Starbucks Idea opens the concept of crowdsourcing to any customer willing to register. But the *Starbucks Ideas In Action* blog, at the Web site, acts as a counterpart to the My Starbucks Idea content. The blog is written by different Starbucks employees and talks about how they implemented an idea or are reacting to the suggestions and information from customers. An interesting aspect of this blog is that readers can provide feedback and comments. Many corporate blogs don't allow that. But by being open to a second level of feedback, Starbucks can continue the dialogue with customers and extend the Starbucks experience *outside* the store.

Did You Know?

You can reuse your content across multiple platforms as long as you don't duplicate it 100 percent across different sites. If you duplicate the content exactly, search engines might think you're trying to spam the system. But repurposed content that borrows from your original content is fine.

Social media is a relatively new medium, but its newness does not preempt the traditional rules of marketing. Whether you're attempting to "sell" yourself as an industry expert or build buzz and kick-start sales of a breakthrough product your company has just developed, you must determine who your likely buyers are, whether they hang out on the social media circuit, and how to generate content that appeals to them.

Embarking on a social media campaign is time consuming and, thus, expensive. Although hitting the Tweet button has virtually no cost, a social media campaign must be planned, nurtured, tracked, and managed with the same vigilance of any other marketing campaign. Social media often allows for an intimate look at your brand, so letting the summer intern run amuck posting on behalf of your organization is probably not the best strategy.

Let's take a quick look at our key concepts and action steps before we move on to the next chapter.

- ▶ **Key concept:** It's critical to have a well-defined brand before you embark on a social media marketing campaign.

- ▶ **Action step:** Perform an audit of your brand to determine whether gaps exist in one of the following places: 1) between what you *are* and what you want to *be,* 2) between what you want to be and how your customers perceive you, and 3) between what you want to be and what you can be based on your organizational resources, structure, and strategy.

▸ **Key concept:** Your social media strategy must align with your brand's essence for your marketing efforts to work together.

▸ **Action step:** Identify key drivers of brand essence and use them to develop your marketing communications strategy. Your social media strategy should also be developed based on this same set of key drivers, to achieve maximum communications impact.

▸ **Key concept:** Brands that are transparent and authentic have a better chance of success with consumers than brands that don't.

▸ **Action step:** Be authentic and transparent 100 percent of the time. No exceptions.

ENDNOTES

1. See www.penn-olson.com/2010/04/20/4-disturbing-social-media-statistics-for-businesses/.

PART V

HOW TO MEASURE SOCIAL MEDIA

WHEN YOU THINK ABOUT IT, THE ONLY TRULY IMPORTANT SOCIAL MEDIA METRIC IS GOOD OLD RETURN ON INVESTMENT (ROI). EVERYTHING ELSE— TRAFFIC, COMMENTS, FOLLOWERS, LEADS—IS JUST A STOP ALONG THE WAY TO ROI.

CHAPTER 20

HOW TO MEASURE A SOCIAL MEDIA CAMPAIGN

Without a positive ROI, there's really no reason to run a social media campaign (unless you're doing it just for kicks). If your social media campaign doesn't have a positive ROI, it won't be long before you get a knock on the door from the CFO or CEO telling you to shut the whole thing down.

It's a good idea to keep ROI on your radar screen at all times. It's easy to get distracted by the minutiae of running a campaign, but ROI should be front and center in everything you do.

One of the ways we keep ROI in our sights is by using something we've come up with called the social media management principle (see Figure 20.1). This simple concept divides social media content into things that are *distractions* and things that are *attractions*.

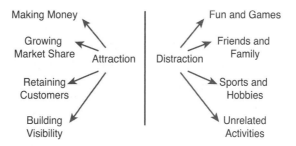

Social Media Management Principle

Figure 20.1 Using the social media management principle keeps you focused on the most important task: making money.

A social media distraction takes you away from the task of generating a positive ROI for your company. Common distractions are articles, videos, and other content that fall into several categories: fun and games, friends and family, sports and hobbies, or other unrelated activities. It's fine to spend time on those kinds of things after hours, but during work, it's best to keep them to a minimum.

On the other hand are social media *attractions,* which can help you improve your social media ROI. They include articles, videos, and other content that help you make money, grow market share, retain customers, or build visibility.

Keep the social media management principle in mind as you run your campaign. It's easy to get distracted when you're running a social media campaign, so be sure to focus on what will help you generate a positive ROI.

SETTING OBJECTIVES FOR YOUR CAMPAIGN

Shortly, we talk about how to *measure* a social media campaign, but first let's cover *setting objectives*. After all, there's no point in measuring anything unless you have a clear set of business objectives in mind.

We've established that the ultimate objective for most social media campaigns is a positive ROI. A positive ROI is the result of converting a prospect to a customer. In Chapter 23, "Step 3: Measuring the Only Really Important Thing—Your Return on Investment," we talk about these objectives in greater detail, but for now, keep these points in mind:

1. **The objective for some social media campaigns is to drive *immediate* sales.** As mentioned previously, Dell Computers uses this model with its DellOutlets Twitter page. The tweets on the DellOutlets page are specifically designed to drive immediate sales.

2. **The objective for some social media campaigns is to drive *future* sales.** The MyStarbucksIdea.com Web site is designed to create Awareness, Interest, Desire, and Action (AIDA). You can't buy a cup of coffee on the MyStarbucksIdea.com Web site—but you sure can build up a desire for one there.

Keep both of these points in mind as you're thinking about your own social media campaign. Be sure to ask yourself, "Do I want do drive sales immediately? Or do I want to build demand for future sales?" They're both important objectives, and they're not mutually exclusive. They're important to keep in mind as you move forward with your campaign.

THE SEVEN DEADLY SINS OF SOCIAL MEDIA MEASUREMENT

The Seven Deadly Sins of Social Media Measurement are the most common mistakes people make in measuring social media. It's a good idea to be aware of these as you move forward. After all, it's sometimes easier to learn from others' mistakes than to learn from their successes.

▶ **Deadly Sin #1: Not measuring your social media campaign**—Not measuring anything around your social media campaign is, well, not very smart. Surprisingly, many people who dive into social media without setting up a plan for measurement. Remember, you need to set your business objectives first and then determine how you're going to measure against those objectives. We think of this as taking a step back before you take a step forward. It's a good approach.

▶ **Deadly Sin #2: Measuring everything**—Social media is primarily digital in nature, so just about anything can be tracked. You can keep an eye on uploads, downloads, ratings, comments, bookmarks, fans, followers, and a slew of other things. But if you don't have a plan behind what you're measuring, you'll end up with too much data. Believe it or not, you can run a successful social media campaign by keeping track of as few as five to ten key metrics.

▶ **Deadly Sin #3: Measuring the wrong thing**—It's easy to get distracted with social media. Many people go on tangents and measure things that don't lead to *making money*. Remember, in our opinion, the only reason to run a social media campaign is to eventually make money, so be sure everything you do points in that direction.

▶ **Deadly Sin #4: Measuring just to measure**—Don't just measure something because you can. After all, there's no point in having information if you don't also have *insight*. Spend some time developing insights using the data you do have. For example, don't just track the data that shows the average person visits only 1.5 pages on your site. Try to understand *why* people visit only 1.5 pages, and then try to get them to increase their page views to 2.0 per visit and more.

▶ **Deadly Sin #5: Not tracking your progress**—If you're taking the time and trouble to measure something, be sure you can compare it to past performance. That way, when you see improvement over time, you can go into the CEO and say, "See? I told you this social media stuff works. Here's proof, Mr. Big Shot." (*Please be advised:* Don't call your CEO "Mr. Big Shot" unless he's a man and you're on very good terms with him.)

▶ **Deadly Sin #6: Not sharing your progress.** Remember the CEO you were calling Mr. Big Shot? Whether or not you call your CEO that, be sure to share your results with all the relevant members of your management team. It's better to overshare than to not share enough. You always want key influencers and decision makers within your company to be aware of your social media successes.

▶ **Deadly Sin #7: There is no seventh deadly sin**—There are only six deadly sins of social media measurement. But if we called this the "Six Deadly Sins of Social Media Measurement," it wouldn't have the same ring to it, so we called it the "Seven Deadly Sins." Can you think of a seventh deadly sin of social media measurement? If so, let us know about it. Just visit 60SecondMarketer.com/ SeventhDeadlySin and add yours to the growing list of social media deadly sins.

Those are the Seven—okay, *Six*—Deadly Sins of Social Media Measurement. Keep them in mind as you set the foundation for your social media measurement program.

SEGMENTING SOCIAL MEDIA MEASUREMENT INTO CATEGORIES

This list includes just some of the things you can measure in a social media campaign. After a while, it gets pretty confusing— and if you tried measuring everything on the list, you'd end up with a lot of *information* but little *insight*. Because of that, we are going to categorize the information into three groups—but first, let's look at a list of *some* of the things you can measure:

- ▶ Twitter followers

- ▶ Facebook fans

- ▶ Comments

- ▶ Social bookmarks

- ▶ Page views

- ▶ Inbound links

- ▶ Click-throughs

- ▶ Leads generated

- ▶ Ratings

- ▶ Downloads

- ▶ Conversions

- ▶ CPM

- ▶ Likes/Favorites

- ▶ Uploads

- ▶ Growth rate of fans, followers, and friends

- ▶ Online mentions across blogs, microblogs, message boards, and so on

- ▶ Geographic distribution of mentions

- ▶ Positive and negative sentiment surrounding your brand

- ▶ Viral video activity

- ▶ Bounce rate

These are just some of the things you can measure in a social media campaign, and you can see by this short list that it can get pretty confusing pretty quickly.

Quick Start Guide

In an effort to take a step back before we take a step forward, let's break things down into three easy steps so you know how to move forward:

Step 1: Measure the quantity. These social media metrics are quantitative in nature. By that, we mean that the metrics simply measure data and have little emotional content. They include the number of Twitter followers, the number of inbound links, the geographic distribution of mentions, the click-through rates, and other items that are data-centric in nature.

Step 2: Measure the quality. These social media metrics are qualitative in nature. They provide information about the emotions, thoughts, and intensity of feelings about your product or service. (For example, having the word *cheap* used to describe your brand is very different than having the word *inexpensive* used.)

Step 3: Measure the ROI. These social media metrics help you track your progress toward your ultimate goal, which is to make money with social media. They include metrics such as leads generated, customers retained, prospects converted, and, most important, profits generated.

In upcoming chapters, we dive deeper into these categories of social media measurement tools. For now, let's do a recap of the key concepts and action steps from this chapter.

- ► **Key concept:** The most important social media metric is your return on investment (ROI).

- ► **Action step:** It's easy to get distracted by other important metrics, but every other metric you measure should ultimately lead to ROI. Always keep your social media ROI on your radar screen.

- ► **Key concept:** The social media management principle is a way to stay focused on social media tools that help you make money, grow market share, retain customers, or build visibility.

▶ **Action step:** Sketch out the social media management principle on a yellow sticky note and attach it to your computer monitor. Seriously, try it. It sounds silly, but it'll keep you focused on the only thing that's important: generating a positive ROI.

▶ **Key concept:** Social media campaigns come in two flavors: those that help you generate immediate sales and those that help you generate future sales.

▶ **Action step:** Figure out which kind of social media campaign you want. Remember, they're not mutually exclusive, so you can have both.

▶ **Key concept:** The Deadly Sins of Social Media Measurement are the most common mistakes people make when measuring their social media campaigns.

▶ **Action step:** Review all Six Deadly Sins of Social Media Measurement and make a recommendation for a seventh deadly sin at 60SecondMarketer.com/SeventhDeadlySin.

▶ **Key concept:** Social media measurement involves following a process. Step 1 measures the quantity. Step 2 measures the quality. Step 3 measures the ROI.

▶ **Action step:** Keep these three categories in mind as you develop your social media campaign. By grouping your social media measurement tools into these categories, you'll be able to stay more organized in your approach.

IN THE PREVIOUS CHAPTER, WE MENTIONED THAT IT'S EASIER TO WRAP YOUR MIND AROUND ALL THE WAYS YOU CAN MEASURE SOCIAL MEDIA IF YOU LAY IT OUT IN THREE DISTINCT STEPS. STEP 1 IS MEASURING THE *QUANTITY*. STEP 2 IS MEASURING THE *QUALITY*. STEP 3 IS MEASURING THE *RETURN ON INVESTMENT (ROI)*.

CHAPTER 21

STEP 1: MEASURING THE QUANTITATIVE DATA

Measuring the *quantity* gives you insight into the volume of traffic your social media campaign is generating. A basic metric for measuring quantity is the number of Twitter followers or Facebook fans you have. That's pretty straightforward.

Measuring the *quality* gives you insight into the emotions, thoughts, and feelings surrounding your brand. By studying the emotional component of your social media campaign, you'll be able to get a sense of how loyal people are to your brand and what inner needs are being fulfilled by your brand's social media campaign.

Measuring the *ROI* is, of course, the most important metric. By analyzing your leads generated, prospects converted, customers retained, and profits generated, you'll be able to track your progress on your ultimate goal, which is to make money with social media.

MEASURING TRAFFIC ON YOUR OWN WEB SITE

We're going to kick off this chapter by talking about Step 1, the *quantitative* measurement of your campaign. Quantitative measurements give you an understanding of how people are engaging with your brand online.

The first and easiest way to get a quantitative measurement of your social media program is to track visits to your Web site using a tool such as Google Analytics, GoingUp!, Coremetrics, or Omniture. All four of these tools provide in-depth information that let you track data involving number of visits, page views, pages per visit, bounce rate, reach, and average time on site.

Did You Know?

The *bounce rate* is the percentage of visitors who "bounce" off your site after visiting only one page. The *reach* is the percent of global Internet users who visit your site.[1]

Here's a quick rundown of these important tools:

▶ **Google Analytics**—What's not to like about Google Analytics? By dropping a line of code into your Web site, you can track how people get to your site, how they navigate through your site, and how long they stay on your site. It has an easy-to-use dashboard that keeps things snappy and efficient. Best of all, it's free.

▶ **GoingUp!**—This Web analytics package helps you track the progress of your online marketing campaign. You can check out your traffic trends, referring keywords, user profile data, and Google Page Rank progress. It has an easy-to-use graphical interface that really enhances the experience of analyzing and understanding large quantities of data.

▶ **Coremetrics**—If you're ready to step it up a notch, you'll want to invest in Coremetrics. It's a Web analytics tool that captures every click by every visitor over time and stores them in a profile database. One of the advantages of Coremetrics is that it can track and measure individual behavior across multiple visits for the entire lifecycle of each visitor. This gives you the ability to customize your prospects' experiences, thereby improving your conversion rate.

▶ **Omniture**—As with Coremetrics, this tool requires an investment. But the added horsepower is perfect if you're interested in getting deep insights into your visitors. Omniture lets you measure trends in customer behavior in real time, allows you to test site design and navigational elements, and provides advanced segmentation and analytics tools to give you a clear understanding of who your customers are and what their needs are.

A wide variety of tools are available to help you track prospect and customer data. But Google Analytics, GoingUp!, Coremetrics, and Omniture are the top tools in this category—you won't go wrong with any of them.

MEASURING TRAFFIC ON YOUR COMPETITORS' WEB SITES

You're probably interested in measuring the traffic to your Web site because it gives you insights into your target market's behavior. Similarly, you should be interested in measuring the traffic to your competitors' Web sites because it gives you insights into their prospects and customers. Both metrics are important but different.

One of the best tools to measure visits to a competitor's blog is Compete.com. The Freemium version is an engaging and powerful tool that lets you check traffic data on competing Web sites. (It's worth noting that Compete.com doesn't track all Web sites—just sites with a reasonable amount of traffic.) Compete.com also lets you compare traffic across a variety of Web sites. So, for example, you could compare the unique monthly visits to AcmePlumbing.com, ZZZPlumbing.com, and AAAPlumbing.com all at once.

Alexa.com is another good tool for measuring traffic. It usually focuses on the very largest Web sites, but it has a number of good features that can come in handy for people interested in measuring the chatter around a specific Web site. Some of these features include the capability to look at traffic statistics, audience information, traffic rank, page views, reach, and bounce rate.

Technorati is another good tool that can track traffic to your site or a competitor's site. It was originally designed to help bloggers by collecting, highlighting, and distributing information about other bloggers. Since then, it has evolved into an online resource for Web site owners but still includes helpful tools that can give you insights into other blogs and Web sites.

MEASURING TRAFFIC ON YOUR SOCIAL MEDIA CHANNELS

Where do most of your YouTube viewers live? What are the demographics of your Facebook fans? And how many people in your LinkedIn group went to Yale? These are just some of the insights you can derive simply by taking a deeper dive into the tools readily available to you—for free, no less—on your existing social media channels.

Next time you're uploading a video to your YouTube channel, go to the My Account link and navigate to your YouTube Insights page. There you'll uncover a wealth of information about your visitors. You'll be able to find out the ages of the people who are looking at your videos, how many are male or female, and the total number of views your videos are getting. You'll even be able to see how *attentive people were when they were watching your videos*. Seriously, YouTube has analytics tools that can tell whether people are doing other activities (such as checking e-mails) while watching your videos. It's scary. And kind of cool. Come to think of it, it's both scary and cool all wrapped up into one.

Facebook has a similar set of tools. Facebook Insights can provide information about your total number of fans, their interactions with the page, and the number of wall posts they've made. It can also provide demographic information such as age and gender. And you can manipulate all of this data on easy-to-use, graphical charts that can quickly give you a snapshot of your visitors and their interactions with your Facebook page.

LinkedIn provides some good information about your connections, but it focuses more on individuals than broad swaths of people. For example, you can find out where one of your connections went to college, where that person worked, and whether he already knows some of the people you know.

LinkedIn is perfect for people in sales who need to get the inside scoop on someone before smiling and dialing. It's not as good for large-scale data analytics.

Other tools are coming online all the time. Some of these tools are designed to give you insights into your visitors and followers on Twitter, Flickr, Vimeo, and other sites, so keep an eye out for them. Most of all, *use them*. There's no point in having access to information unless you're going to derive insights from your data.

MEASURING YOUR ONLINE MENTIONS ACROSS DIFFERENT PLATFORMS

Are you interested in finding out what people are saying about your brand across blogs, microblogs, message boards, wikis, and video-sharing sites? That's not as difficult as it once was. Today tools such as Alterian SM2, Spiral16, Google Alerts, and SocialMention can help you do that.

Here's a quick rundown of these tools:

- ▶ **Alterian SM2**—This robust and engaging Web tool provides insights into what people are saying online about your brand, your competitors' brands, or just about any other topic you choose. SM2 provides data and information about the volume of mentions, the share of voice, the demographics, the content tone, and the content emotions. You can even set it up so that it e-mails you a customized report at the end of each day.

▶ **Spiral16**—If you're a visual person, Spiral16 may be just what you're looking for. It's a Web-based platform that helps you listen, measure, and visualize your brand's online presence. You can measure the impact your traditional campaigns have on your social media campaigns and understand why consumers are behaving the way they are. It's a data-centric platform that uses graphics to quickly and efficiently help you spot trends and react to them in real time.

▶ **Google Alerts**—If you're not already using Google Alerts, put down the book and go to Google.com/alerts to set it up. It takes about two minutes to type in several keywords and then get daily e-mails letting you know what was said about those keywords and where. For example, you'll want to set up your Google Alerts to tell you when someone has mentioned your brand or your competitors' brands online. You can even set it up to alert you to topical mentions such as "marketing tips" or *How to Make Money with Social Media.*

▶ **SocialMention**—This tool is similar to Search.Twitter. com, in that it provides data and information about certain keywords and how they're used online. Interested in finding out what people are saying about Toyota right now? Stop by SocialMention.com and find out. It's a good tool that can provide some quick information on just about any term that strikes your fancy.

OTHER QUANTITATIVE METRICS

You'll want to keep track of other important metrics as you grow your social media campaign. Here's a quick rundown of some of them:

- ▶ Social bookmarks
- ▶ Inbound links to your Web site
- ▶ Click-throughs on your Web site
- ▶ Likes/Favorites on Facebook
- ▶ E-book downloads
- ▶ User-initiated reviews
- ▶ Ratings
- ▶ Traffic generated by earned media vs. free media
- ▶ Participation in polls
- ▶ Contest entries
- ▶ New e-newsletter subscribers
- ▶ E-newsletter unsubscribers

The Big Idea

By breaking down your data into these distinct categories, you'll be able to develop key insights around each set of data:

- ▶ Traffic on your own Web site
- ▶ Traffic on your competitors' sites
- ▶ Traffic on the social media channels you own

- ▶ Comments about your brand, your competitors' brands, or other topics on social media channels you don't own

- ▶ Inbound links, ratings, e-book downloads, and other relevant metrics

The bottom line is that social media provides a wealth of information for anyone who wants to spend a few minutes tracking it down. The problem isn't a lack of data; the problem is that there's *too much data*. By breaking down your data down into several distinct categories, it's easier to wrap your mind around it and keep track of the insights derived from it.

With that in mind, let's recap some of the key concepts and action steps from this chapter.

- ▶ **Key concept:** You can measure a wide range of quantitative data on your social media campaign, including traffic to your site, traffic to your competitors' sites, and traffic on social media channels you own.

- ▶ **Action step:** Break down your data into groups so that you can wrap your mind around the information and develop insights from it.

- ▶ **Key concept:** You can track comments about your brand, your competitors' brands, and your industry by using a few simple tools, such as Alterian SM2, Spiral16, Google Alerts, and SocialMention.

- ▶ **Action step:** Don't use all of these tools, or you'll be overwhelmed. Your best bet is to start with Google Alerts and then add one other tool on top of that.

▶ **Key concept:** Some important quantitative metrics fall outside the groups we've broken out here. They include e-book downloads, inbound links to your Web site, user-generated ratings, and other data.

▶ **Action step:** Figure out three to six additional metrics you'd like to keep track of. Even though these metrics fall outside of the nice, tidy little groupings we've created, it doesn't mean that they aren't important. You should still keep tabs on them.

ENDNOTES

1. See www.google.com/support/analytics/bin/answer.py?hl=en&answer=81986; http://gigaom.com/2010/03/17/sequoias-kvamme-social-media-marketing-can-replace-advertising/.

IN THE PREVIOUS CHAPTER, WE DISCUSSED SOME OF THE TOOLS AND TECHNIQUES YOU NEED TO MAKE QUANTITATIVE MEASUREMENTS IN YOUR SOCIAL MEDIA CAMPAIGN. THESE INCLUDE YOUR NUMBER OF TWITTER FOLLOWERS, THE NUMBER OF COMMENTS ABOUT YOUR BRAND ON INDUSTRY FORUMS, AND YOUR BOUNCE RATE ON YOUR WEB SITE.

CHAPTER 22

STEP 2: MEASURING THE
QUALITATIVE DATA

All these are important metrics, but they're just the first step to getting an in-depth and complete understanding of the effectiveness of your campaign. Quantitative data is important, but so is *qualitative* data.

USING QUALITATIVE DATA TO GET INSIGHTS FROM YOUR CUSTOMERS

What is qualitative data? It's the data that gives you insight into the emotions, thoughts, or feelings people have surrounding your brand. You can gain a lot of insight into your brand and how people perceive it by studying what people are saying about it online. Previously, we mentioned that if people say your product is "inexpensive," it has a much different meaning than if they said it was "cheap." And if someone said your YouTube video was "funny," that would be much better than if they said it was "laughable."

You can get qualitative data about your social media campaign in two primary ways. The first is to use tools readily available on the Internet to "listen in" on people's public conversations about your brand online. The second is to ask people directly by using inbound and outbound surveys.

Let's start by talking about inbound and outbound surveys. As you know, a survey is a tool you can use to get data and insights into people's impressions of your brand. With an inbound survey, prospects and customers have come to you and stumbled upon a survey tool or button on your site. With an outbound survey, you've reached out to prospects and customers and asked them to participate in your survey.

Did You Know?

Most people fall into the trap of measuring just the *quantitative* data about their campaign, but the deepest insights are often found in the *qualitative* data.

Three popular tools for inbound surveys on your blog or Web site include UserVoice, Kampyle, and Get Satisfaction. You may have seen these tools on a few blogs or Web sites you've visited. Typically, they include a tab or button located on the site that, once clicked, provides a short survey or forum for visitors to provide useful feedback.

Here's a quick rundown of each platform:

- ▶ **UserVoice** is easy to install and directs people to a forum where they can provide tips, hints, and suggestions about your product or service. It's primarily used to allow open-ended feedback in a forum environment.

- ▶ **Kampyle** allows you to drop a line of code into your Web site that places a feedback tab on one of the corners of your site. Visitors see the feedback form and can provide short suggestions, compliments, or input on their experience with your brand, Web site, or blog.

> ▶ **Get Satisfaction** allows feedback from prospects and customers across a variety of other venues, including Facebook and WordPress. Users can ask a question, share an idea, report a problem, or give praise. You also get the ability to respond to their input.

You can expand the scope of your inbound survey by creating an entire Web site designed to generate feedback. As discussed earlier, Starbucks has done this with the MyStarbucksIdea.com Web site. It gives people an opportunity to share their ideas for improving Starbucks with others, and can then vote on their favorites, discuss which ones they like the best, and see the results of their feedback. It's a robust Web site with great links and pages, definitely worth checking out.

Outbound surveys are surveys that you create and send to customers and prospects. The best and easiest way to send out an outbound survey is via e-mail, using a tool such as ConstantContact, ExactTarget, or iContact. Be sure you follow CAN-SPAM guidelines when you're using any of these tools to conduct outbound surveys. Many have a "one strike and you're out" policy when it comes to misusing e-mail lists.

CREATING YOUR OWN SURVEY

What are some questions you might want to ask in an inbound and outbound survey? How should you write the questions? And what can you learn from someone who didn't buy your product or service?

Consider a few tips on creating a survey, to help you get started:

- ▶ Introduce only one issue for every question. If the issue is complex, divide it into several questions.

- ▶ Make sure your questions are crisp and clear. Test them on business associates first, to ensure that there's no room for misinterpretation.

- ▶ Are you interested in finding out whether your customers are satisfied? Some customer satisfaction questions include "How satisfied were you with your purchase?" and "How satisfied were you with your customer service?" and "How satisfied were you with our company overall?"

- ▶ Are you interested in finding out whether your customers are loyal? Some customer loyalty questions include "How likely are you to buy from us again?" and "How likely are you to recommend our product/service to others?" and "How likely are you to recommend our company to others?"

- ▶ Remember, surveys aren't just about information; they're about insights. What trends have you spotted? Do they vary by region? What are the demographics of the people responding to your survey? What unspoken insights can you derive from the data? Don't just look at the data—try to draw actionable insights from it.

- ▶ You'll learn more from a lost prospect than from a gained customer. If you can contact prospects who didn't buy your product or service, ask them why they didn't buy it. Find out if they can articulate what drove them away.

Sometimes the answers will surprise you: "I didn't like your logo." Other times, the answers will frustrate you: "Your salesperson didn't return my call."

LISTENING TO THE ONLINE CONVERSATION

We have some good news. When someone makes a comment about your brand on a blog post, a forum, a Twitter account, a Facebook page, or just about any other social media platform, that's public information. It's as if they stood on a street corner with a megaphone and announced to the world that they're a fan (or not) of your product or service.

We have some better news. Plenty of wonderful tools are available for monitoring those conversations. Some of them are free. The best ones cost money. But if you're a company that's interested in getting insights into your customers and prospects, these tools are a great way to do that.

But wait—it gets even better. Some of these tools actually do some of the work for you. After all, if you downloaded a slew of comments about your brand, you'd be overwhelmed pretty quickly. The best tools allow you to derive insights into the sentiment associated with comments about your brand. That way, you can get a deeper understanding about people's thoughts and feelings about your brand.

The Big Idea

Quantitative data gives you a snapshot of the state of your social media campaign. Qualitative data provides you deeper insights about your customers' needs and wants.

We discussed several tools in the previous chapter that help measure the quantitative data surrounding your social media campaign. Some of those tools can also measure the qualitative data surrounding your social media conversation. In other words, they can give you insights into the meaning behind the conversations.

Here's a quick rundown on some of the most important tools on that front:

> ▶ **Nielsen BuzzMetrics**—This tool is especially good for big brands with big budgets. BuzzMetrics monitors data from nearly 100 million blogs, social networks, groups, boards, and other consumer-generated media platforms. It allows you to listen to customer conversations, monitor and analyze how customers are discussing your brand online, gain an understanding of what customers think about your new product concepts, and discover how your online and offline marketing campaigns resonate with customers.

> ▶ **Social Radar**—This tool enables you to track, measure, analyze, and understand chatter from all over the Web. You can track a new product launch, measure the response of an ad campaign, listen to the thoughts and opinions of consumers, analyze buzz, and review where to target your

ads and social efforts. You can even measure and track mentions of any topic during any time range, dating back several years. Best of all, you can measure the sentiment of conversations and learn what's causing the emotions behind the comments.

▶ **Rapleaf**—This tool is slightly different than the two already mentioned. BuzzMetrics and Social Radar monitor the chatter online and allow you to derive insights from that data. With Rapleaf, you reverse-append existing data, such as e-mail addresses, to match social media profiles. In other words, you can use your e-mail database and, based on existing profiles on LinkedIn, Facebook, and other social media platforms, derive insights into the wants, needs, and desires of your existing pool of customers and prospects.

▶ **Radian6**—This Web-based platform enables you to monitor the online chatter about your brand. It's set up to be easy to use and to provide ways to quickly discuss insights with other team members in your company. You can share information with customer service, sales, product, and executive teams to coordinate responses, notify team members of emerging issues, or keep account teams apprised of new details related to the comments. Overall, it's a robust platform that combines power with ease of use.

▶ **Alterian SM2**—This tool provides data and information about the volume of mentions, the share of voice, the demographics, and the tone and the emotions of the comments about your brand that happen online.

▶ **Spiral16**—This tool can help you listen, measure, and visualize your brand's online presence. You can even measure the impact your traditional campaigns have on your social media campaigns and understand why customers are behaving the way they are.

That should give you a quick snapshot of some of the better tools available to measure the qualitative nature of your social media campaign. New tools are coming online all the time, so don't hesitate to do a search on "social media monitoring tools" or "how to measure online."

MISTAKES TO AVOID WHEN MEASURING QUALITATIVE SOCIAL MEDIA DATA

People do three things wrong when they set up a qualitative social media measurement program. By keeping these three on your radar screen, you can avoid shooting yourself in the foot:

1. **Gathering too much data**—It's tempting to gather reams of data about your social media campaign, but a better solution is to start small, with just a few sets of data. Wrap your mind around those and watch for trends. When you've got a handle on those sets of data, add one or two more. Rinse and repeat.

2. **Not sharing the data**—If you're in marketing, you'll be looking at the data with a different set of eyes than someone in sales. Ditto for someone in the C-level

suite. Remember that sharing data isn't about spewing spreadsheets around the office. It's about providing data along with insights about that data. When you share insights, you're allowing others to build upon your initial input. That's good for you and your company.

3. **Not acting upon the data**—This is another all-too-common problem. People forget that data is just data until you do something with it. If you're presenting a report, be sure you end the report with action steps based on the data.

With that said, let's talk about the key concepts and action steps from this chapter.

▶ **Key concept:** You can use two kinds of social media surveys to gather actionable data from customers and prospects: inbound and outbound.

▶ **Action step:** Decide which kind of survey is best for your purposes. In some cases, you want to incorporate both inbound and outbound surveys to get the best results.

▶ **Key concept:** A number of good tools enable you to monitor the social media chatter about your company online.

▶ **Action step:** Use one of the tools to gather data. But use your most important tool, your brain, to derive insights from the data.

▶ **Key concept:** The three most common mistakes to avoid when monitoring social media qualitative data are

1) gathering too much data, 2) not sharing the data, and 3) not acting upon the data.

▶ **Action step:** Of these three, the most egregious crime is not acting upon the data. What's the point of gathering data if you're not going to act upon it. Get acting, will ya?

WE'VE TALKED ABOUT WHERE MARKETING HAS BEEN AND WHERE IT'S GOING. NOW IT'S TIME TO TALK ABOUT SOMETHING THAT'S IMPORTANT RIGHT NOW: YOUR RETURN ON INVESTMENT (ROI). AFTER ALL, THE ONLY REAL REASON YOU'RE SETTING UP, RUNNING, AND MANAGING A SOCIAL MEDIA CAMPAIGN IS TO MAKE MONEY, RIGHT?

CHAPTER 23

STEP 3: MEASURING THE ONLY REALLY IMPORTANT THING— YOUR RETURN ON INVESTMENT

UNDERSTANDING CUSTOMER LIFETIME VALUE

Before we dive into ROI, let's talk about an important concept called Customer Lifetime Value. **Customer Lifetime Value (CLV),** is the amount of revenue you'll generate from one customer during the lifetime of your relationship.

For example, let's assume that you're a cable TV provider who knows that the average customer spends $100 a month on your service. In 12 months you generate $1,200 from the typical customer. But that customer doesn't stay with you for just 12 months. He stays with you for 3.5 years, which means that his Customer Lifetime Value is $4,200 ($100 per month × 12 months × 3.5 years).

The next step is to figure out how much money you'd spend to acquire that customer. Many chief marketing officers (and chief financial officers) believe that 10 percent of CLV is a good estimate. So in the example of the cable company, you might spend approximately $420 in marketing costs to gain a new customer. That's considered your allowable **cost per acquisition (CPA),** which is sometimes called **cost per sale (CPS).**

Many companies spend a lot of time analyzing their CLV and their CPA. On the low end of the scale, you might have a software company that sells its software for $49. Its customers might purchase the software only once every two years, and they might repurchase it only when it contains a significant upgrade. In this example, the company's CLV is just $49 (because customers repurchase only when it contains a significant upgrade), which leaves *just $4.90 for the company's allowable CPA.*

On the other end of the spectrum might be a car company that sells a model for $40,000. If the average customer buys 2.5 cars from the car company before switching brands, that's a CLV of $100,000 and an allowable CPA of $10,000—not bad.

The bottom line is that you can use multiple approaches to calculate CLV and CPA. The examples mentioned previously start you with a good, basic formula for understanding the metrics of your social media ROI.

USING SOCIAL MEDIA FOR CUSTOMER RETENTION PURPOSES

A general rule of thumb for most businesses is that *it costs three to five times as much to get a new customer as it does to keep an existing one.* That's part of the reason most corporations focus so much time and money on customer retention—it pays to keep existing customers happy.

For example, say you're The Home Depot and there's a Lowe's across the street from you. (This is not as unusual as you might think.) You'd probably spend a great deal of money training your employees on everything they need to know about customer retention. If it costs three to five times as much to acquire a new customer as it does to prevent an existing one from leaving, it would be smart to focus time and money on keeping the existing customer satisfied.

Another great example of this is the Comcast cable company. It has a number of formidable competitors, ranging from AT&T to DirecTV. Comcast, AT&T, and DirecTV all know their CLV and their CPA. And they spend a lot of money training their customer service representatives on how to keep and maintain their existing customers.

That's exactly what was crossing Frank Eliason's mind when he was taking a spin around Twitter one day and noticed that some of Comcast's existing customers were venting their frustrations about Comcast on Twitter. As a longstanding employee of Comcast, the odds were pretty good that Eliason knew Comcast's CLV and that he also understood how hard it is for any corporation to get new customers. So when Eliason saw people venting their frustrations with Comcast on Twitter, it hit pretty close to home.

The good news (for Eliason, anyway) is that he knew he could solve a lot of the customers' issues remotely. For example, when a customer loses Internet connection, the solution is often to turn off the modem and then turn it back on again. Half the people tweeting their frustrations were complaining about their Internet connection, and Eliason realized that he could fix the problem via Twitter (for example, "Hey, @60SecondTweets—if you're having problems with your connection, turn off your modem and then turn it back on again. If that doesn't work, call us at 1-800-COMCAST.")

Let's assume that Comcast's CLV is the $4,200 that we mentioned in the previous cable example. (That's a guess, but it's probably not far off.) The allowable CPA in that calculation is $420. If it costs three to five times as much to get a new customer as it does to keep an existing one, then Eliason knows that every time he prevents a customer from leaving Comcast to go to DirecTV, he's saving his company between $1,260 and $2,100.

Now before you run to your CFO with these figures, you should note a few things. First, we don't know for sure that Comcast's CLV is $420. Second, the cost to get a new customer varies by industry, so the three to five times figure might be different for your company. Third, not everyone who complains on Twitter about Comcast goes to a competitor. (In fact, only a small percentage do.) However, these metrics *can* give you an idea of how to create a model to calculate the ROI of one aspect of your social media program.

The Big Idea

If you know your CLV and your allowable CPA, you'll be in a good position to calculate the ROI of your social media program.

GENERATING LEADS WITH SOCIAL MEDIA

Many companies sell their products over the Internet on e-commerce sites. It works successfully for 1-800-Flowers, iTunes, and OverStock.com. But what if you don't sell products online? What if you're Roto-Rooter, a car dealership, or a real estate agent? If you're in one of these businesses, you're interested in generating *leads.*

A **lead** is an inbound prospect who is interested in your product or service (or your competitor's product or service). If you can capture a lead and nurture it through the sales funnel, you can convert that prospect into a customer. And that means revenue for your company.

The challenge many people face when they use social media to generate leads is that they don't go the final mile. They use social media to build awareness and generate demand for their products or services, but they don't know how to take the final step and turn it into a viable lead.

One of the best ways to use social media to generate leads is to become an *information station* for people in your target market. That's what BKV Digital and Direct Response did with the 60 Second Marketer.

As we've mentioned, BKV is a marketing communications firm that develops highly measurable marketing programs for corporations such as AT&T, Six Flags, the American Red Cross, and Caterpillar. The idea for the 60 Second Marketer started with an analysis of BKV's target market, which is comprised of marketing directors working at large corporations throughout the world.

If you get inside the mind of the typical marketing director at these corporations, you find someone who is very busy and interested in staying abreast of the latest tools, tips, and techniques in marketing. BKV estimated that marketing directors download two to three marketing white papers a month, but they have time to read only a couple of pages of those white papers. The rest get stacked on their desk—unread—and then get tossed in the trash about once every three months.

But what if you could distill those white papers to their essence? What if you could put the most important information into a short, 60-second video that gave the marketing director the key bits of information about the new tool, tip, or technique?

BKV did that with the 60 Second Marketer. BKV set it up to be an information station for marketing directors and, in the process, to introduce them to BKV Digital and Direct Response. BKV nurtured the leads captured through the 60 Second Marketer until the company could convert them into clients through the sales funnel.

The 60 Second Marketer uses a hub-and-spoke system to drive prospects to the Web site and to capture their attention. When prospects sign up for the e-newsletter, participate in a free Webinar, or attend a 60 Second Marketer event, they get subtle, long-term exposure to BKV. The result is an engaged and loyal prospect base, some of whom convert to customers.

You can do the same with your social media campaign. As soon as you've finished this chapter (and not a moment before), we recommend that you sketch out a hub-and-spoke of your own and use it as a way to analyze which social media tools you will use to capture lead data for your business.

CONVERTING LEADS INTO CUSTOMERS

What should you do when you've captured the lead data for your customer prospects? You should start remarketing to them to close the loop. A lead is just a lead until you actively pursue it and convert it to a customer.

This requires good, old-fashioned hard work. Your parents and grandparents used a telephone to connect with prospects for their businesses. They also used sales letters. E-mail is another good tool to convert prospects into customers. The only difference is that your grandparents (and, perhaps, your parents) didn't use it.

A lead doesn't count for anything until you do the hard work to convert it to a sale. That's the final mile, and it's probably the hardest mile. But executing that last mile differentiates the social media wannabes from the social media superstars.

TRACKING YOUR SOCIAL MEDIA ROI

In Chapter 20, "How to Measure a Social Media Campaign," we mention that the only truly important social media metric is ROI. Everything else—traffic, comments, followers, leads—is just a stop along the way.

In this chapter, we've covered a lot of important concepts, including CLV, CPA, lead generation, and prospect conversion.

If you understand those concepts, the rest is just a matter of tracking the data and using it to improve your results.

Most people are familiar with an old question: If a tree falls in the woods and nobody is there, does it still make a sound? The same question holds true for social media: If a social media campaign isn't measured, is it effective?

The answer is "no." A social media campaign that isn't measured isn't effective because you can't tell whether it worked.

The specifics of measuring a social media campaign vary with every company, but let's use a basic example to illustrate the approach. Let's say that you're a lawn care company, and your typical customer spends $80 per month on your service and stays with you for three years. That gives you a CLV of $2,880 and an allowable CPA of $288.

In the past, you might have used direct mail as your primary tool to generate leads and convert those leads into sales. If the conversion rate on your direct mail campaigns was 0.5 percent, you'd have to send out 200 direct mail pieces to acquire a customer. If your printing, postage, list, and marketing costs for those direct mail pieces was $1.44 each, the math works out perfectly to $288. You're golden.

But let's say that the CEO and CFO decide to test a social media campaign against the existing direct mail campaign. Now the math gets kind of interesting. Let's assume that you spend $2.4 million each year to send out two million direct mail pieces that generate 10,000 new customers each year (2 million direct mail pieces × 0.5% = 10,000 new customers). If your annual revenue per customer is $960, that's $9.6 million in incremental revenue each year from new customers. (Don't forget that you have some customer churn, so some of the $9.6 million replaces revenue from lost customers.)

You want to test your social media campaign against your direct mail campaign. If you spend $2.4 million each year on your direct mail campaign, a safe bet would be to spend 10 percent of that, or $240,000, on a test social media campaign.

The costs associated with setting up, launching, and running a social media campaign are often underestimated. Because you don't have media costs for using Twitter, YouTube, Facebook, LinkedIn, or other social media platforms, people often assume that running a social media campaign is cheap. But the manpower involved in running a social media campaign can be significant. So can the costs for producing the content for your social media campaign.

If you're a large company with a brand to protect, you need to create top-notch landing pages on your Web site. That costs money. So do well-produced YouTube videos and effective Facebook promotions.

The point is, you need to dive deep into some of the hidden costs of social media to get a good, clear understanding of your campaign's ROI. In this example, we said that you have $240,000 to spend on labor and production costs. For that $240,000 investment to match the ROI of the direct mail campaign, it would have to generate 1,000 new customers.

That's not as easy as it looks, but it's also not impossible. One of your objectives might be to drive 100,000 people to your landing pages via your social media campaign. Assuming that you were able to do that, it's reasonable to calculate that 1,000 of those would convert to customers, which would match your direct mail campaign dollar for dollar. From that point on, it's simply a matter of testing ways to grow your inbound traffic and to improve your conversion rate.

THE BOTTOM LINE

The most important thing that you can do is track your campaign to the level of prospect conversion. When you're tracking data at that level, you can calculate your ROI. And assuming that the ROI is positive, you can grow your campaign and improve efficiencies over time. And that, friends, translates into profits.

- ▶ **Key concept:** Customer Lifetime Value (CLV) is the revenue you'll generate from a typical customer during the lifetime of your engagement.

- ▶ **Action step**—Calculate your CLV using this simple formula: Monthly revenue × 12 months × Average customer lifecycle = CLV

▶ **Key concept:** Allowable cost per acquisition (CPA) is the amount of money you would spend to acquire a new customer.

▶ **Action step:** Determine your allowable CPA by calculating 10 percent of your CLV.

▶ **Key concept:** Leads or prospects generate $0 for your company until you convert them into a customer.

▶ **Action step:** Embrace the idea that a social media campaign is useless unless you convert your leads and prospects into customers. Track your data to the prospect conversion level, to generate a clear sense of your actual ROI.

PART VI
CONCLUSION

IF YOU'RE A REAL ESTATE AGENT, AN INTERIOR DESIGNER, OR A LANDSCAPE COMPANY, MAKING THE DECISION TO SET UP, RUN, AND MANAGE A SOCIAL MEDIA CAMPAIGN CAN BE PRETTY SIMPLE. ONLY A HANDFUL OF PEOPLE HAVE TO BUY INTO THE CONCEPT, AND WITH A LITTLE PLANNING AND STRATEGIZING, YOU CAN BE OFF TO THE RACES PRETTY QUICKLY.

CHAPTER 24

SOCIAL MEDIA GUIDELINES FOR CORPORATIONS

But if you work at a larger corporation, getting buy-in is only part of the challenge. Invariably, you'll be asked to set up a series of *social media guidelines* for the 10 or 100 or 1,000 people who are going to be helping you execute your program.

With that in mind, we asked Ann Pruitt with the 60 Second Marketer to help us compile a list of guiding principles for large to midsize corporations that want to encourage their employees to take part in using social media. Her goal was to provide guidelines that gave employees clear boundaries but didn't hem them in so much that they would feel overly constricted or limited.

Remember, as our friend Erik Qualman states in his book *Socialnomics,* "What happens in Vegas, stays on YouTube." With that in mind, the last thing your corporation wants is for a random comment or inappropriate conversation to make its way across the social media sphere. It's the quickest way we know to dampen the effects of a successful social media campaign. But at the same time, it's important to recognize that the snowball effect of social media can really work only when employees are given the freedom to respond openly and quickly on any of your social media channels.

Let's take a look at five core values that we've compiled as guiding principles for your company's social media program. These values are based on research we've done into the ways companies such as Dell and The Coca-Cola Company conduct their social media campaigns.

THE FIVE CORE VALUES OF SOCIAL MEDIA BEHAVIOR

All employees who are asked to participate in social media dialogues should embrace the following core values:

▶ **Show respect**—The people on the other end of your social media dialogue are human, too. They have feelings, emotions, and points of view just like you do. Treat them like your neighbors (or, at least, like the neighbors you're friends with).

▶ **Show responsibility**—Take initiative to be trustworthy. If you've been assigned to the social media team, that means you've been given a certain level of responsibility. Honor that responsibility by taking it seriously.

▶ **Demonstrate integrity**—Show sound, moral character. Pretend your grandmother is watching you. After all, she probably is, from somewhere.

▶ **Be ethical**—Be right and honest in your conduct. If you find yourself doing something that you can't be totally transparent about, it's probably not the right thing to do.

▶ **Add value**—Move the ball forward in all your conversations. Provide an insight, a point of view, or something helpful in each one of your interactions. Every time you move the ball forward an inch, you're helping your company achieve its goals.

Now let's drill down a bit and look at 17 guiding principles that fall under these five core values.

17 SOCIAL MEDIA PRINCIPLES FOR CORPORATIONS

Under each value outlined in the last section, you'll find several guiding principles that encourage your employees to be responsible in all your social media initiatives.

Show Respect

1. **Respect property.** Show respect for the opinions and property of your company and of others. Give credit when appropriate, get permission when needed.

2. **Respect privacy.** Any information gathered or personal identifiers collected about customers should not be published or misused irresponsibly. There are no exceptions to this rule.

3. **Respect copyrights and trademarks.** Do not post another company's trademarks or any copyrighted material belonging to another company without getting approval first.

Show Responsibility

4. **Accept personal responsibility.** You post it, you accept the consequences.

5. **Demonstrate admirable online behavior.** Express yourself, but remember anything you say lives forever on

the Internet. Comply with any regulations that govern your site.

6. **Conscientiously represent your company.** Everything you say as a member of the company represents the company. Likewise, writing harshly about your company can have repercussions for you, obviously, when your company gets the news. If internal issues arise within your business, keep them internal.

7. **Mix personal and business lives carefully.** Remember, everything you post on your personal Facebook or My Space could get back to the company.

Demonstrate Integrity

8. **Show transparency.** If you work for a company, you should reveal that information when commenting about that company or its competition.

9. **Use good judgment.** Share your opinions online, but avoid anything that could be considered poor taste; it reflects poorly on you and your company. Certainly avoid anything that could be considered illegal.

10. **Provide a framework for your arguments.** Provide background to support your postings. Arguments that are thoughtful and that go beyond "xx sucks" make your point-of-view more valid.

Be Ethical

11. Protect the company's proprietary information. You are obligated by your contract to protect vital company information, and state laws govern trade secrets.

12. Don't forget your day job. It's important to maintain productivity at your job and not get lost in cyberspace. Realize that customer service may best be handled through social media, but avoiding your work to post an opinion about the new company dress code doesn't add value.

13. Let the experts be the experts. Your readers may have questions on specific products or services about which you have limited knowledge. Forward those questions for the experts to respond to. The same holds true for PR issues.

14. Post truthful information. Do your research to ensure that you aren't just spreading rumors. Correct errors if you find them later.

Add Value

15. Provide value for customers. Social media should bring customers closer to the products and services you sell. Ranting on Facebook about the way Shipping messes everything up makes you look petty and provides no value for the customers. The same holds true for not responding to customers' comments.

16. **Monitor your social media sites.** Posting a Facebook page and then not monitoring it defeats the purpose and is not social media participation. Online sources must be nurtured though active monitoring and participation.

17. **Remember the audience.** Don't forget that readers include clients—past, present, and future—and employees. Don't publish anything that would insult or otherwise alienate these people.

PUT THESE GUIDELINES IN PLACE SOONER RATHER THAN LATER

The Internet is rife with stories from companies or individuals who wish they'd followed these guidelines. One of the more notable is Domino's Pizza, a company that spends tens of millions of dollars each year building and nurturing its brand.

Unfortunately, several rogue employees at a Domino's franchise in North Carolina decided to post a prank YouTube video of some unsanitary and disgusting food-preparation practices. The viral nature of the Internet helped the video generate a million views within days of being uploaded. Worse still, for a short while, Google had five different links on its first page highlighting the video.

It's unfortunate that a few irresponsible employees at a small franchise can do so much damage to a business that has spent so much time and money building a deservedly good reputation. But social media doesn't care how many years you've spent building a brand, even when what's posted on YouTube is false.

Domino's isn't the only company that has had to deal with these kinds of challenges. Not long ago, an employee of a large, well-respected public relations firm was flying to Memphis, Tennessee, to discuss, of all things, *social media* with one of the firm's largest clients, Fed Ex. Unfortunately, this employee, who, as a social media expert, should have known better, decided to tweet his disdain for the city of Memphis just as he was exiting the city's airport.

Twenty minutes later, as he was entering the FedEx headquarters, all hell had broken loose. A number of FedEx employees who followed this gentleman on Twitter saw his tweet about Memphis and, as proud residents of said city, took offense.

Within days, the story had spread across the globe, embarrassing the employee and the PR agency, and bringing into question FedEx's wisdom for hiring a social media expert who assumed nobody was reading his tweets.

Of course, it's easy to look back on other people's missteps and to use 20/20 hindsight to critique their actions and responses. That's actually not our intent with these stories. Our intent is to use these illustrations to highlight the importance of putting some social media guidelines in place as you roll out your social media program.

Let's take a look at some of the key concepts and action steps from this chapter before we move on to the next chapter for a step-by-step action plan for a social media campaign.

- ▶ **Key concept:** As Erik Qualman says, "What happens in Vegas, stays on YouTube."

- ▶ **Action step:** Help employees understand that once a comment, video, or dialogue is posted on the Internet, it's very hard, if not impossible, to make it disappear.

- ▶ **Key concept:** All employees should follow 5 core values and 17 principles if they're going to participate in a corporate social media campaign.

- ▶ **Action step:** Review the 5 core values and 17 principles with all the employees who will be part of the social media team. It sounds like a goofy thing to do, but it'll help them understand that you're taking this seriously.

- ▶ **Key concept:** Companies such as Domino's and FedEx have had their share of negative experiences with social media.

- ▶ **Action step:** If it can happen to Domino's and FedEx, it can happen to you. Be proactive and incorporate these guidelines into your corporate DNA today.

WE'VE COVERED A LOT OF IMPORTANT INFORMATION IN THE PAST FEW HUNDRED PAGES. YOU MIGHT HAVE JOTTED DOWN A FEW NOTES IN THE MARGINS, OR YOU MIGHT HAVE REVIEWED AND TAKEN ACTION ON SOME OF THE KEY CONCEPTS AND ACTION STEPS AT THE END OF EVERY CHAPTER. BUT SOMETIMES IT HELPS TO HAVE A SINGLE CHAPTER WITH A LONG CHECKLIST OF TASKS THAT YOU'LL NEED IN ORDER TO HAVE A SUCCESSFUL SOCIAL MEDIA CAMPAIGN.

CHAPTER 25

59 Things You Need to Do on Your Way to a Successful Social Media Campaign

That's what this chapter is for. It doesn't cover every task we've discussed in the previous chapters, but it should give you a starting point from which you can launch your campaign.

So here goes. Put a check mark next to each task as you complete it. Before you know it, you'll be well on your way to generating real money from your social media campaign.

The preliminaries:

❏ I've conducted a review of my company's *business* and understand its mission, goals, and objectives.

❏ I've conducted a review of my company's *sales program* and understand how a prospect is brought into the sales funnel and converted into a customer.

❏ I've conducted a review of my company's *marketing program* and understand the role the marketing program plays in the overall success of the company.

❏ I've conducted a review of the strategies, tactics, and tools involved in a social media campaign and understand the role each of those strategies, tactics, and tools plays in a well-run social media program.

❏ After doing all of this, I've asked myself, "Is social media right for my company?" If I've concluded that it is, I've moved on to the next steps,

The competitive landscape:

❏ I've reviewed the *overall strengths and weaknesses* of my company's top five competitors.

❑ I've reviewed the *sales and marketing* efforts of my top five competitors.

❑ I've analyzed the specific *social media campaigns* being conducted by my top five competitors.

❑ I've created a list of social media strategies and tactics my competitors are using that appear to be *effective.*

❑ I've created a list of social media strategies and tactics my competitors are using that appear to be *ineffective.*

❑ I've joined my competitor's LinkedIn groups, Facebook pages, YouTube channels, Twitter accounts, and other social media member sites.

❑ I've set up Google Web Alerts and Blog Alerts to send me notifications any time my competitor, my industry, or my company is mentioned in blogs or articles online.

The internal management team:

❑ I've asked the social media proponents in my organization to be advocates for my program. I've asked them to be engaged in any way they can to help my social media program succeed.

❑ I've identified people within my organization who might not be social media advocates and have begun a program to help them understand the value a well-run social media program can bring to our company.

❑ I've assembled a team to help me set up, run, and manage the social media program for my company.

❑ I've asked each team member to buy *How to Make Money with Social Media* to ensure that we're all working from the same playbook.

❑ I've asked each team member to buy *How to Make Money with Social Media* and to give copies to their friends, neighbors, relatives, acquaintances, and complete strangers because I think *everyone* should know this stuff.

Setting up for success:

❑ I've assembled a social media team to help me execute my program. (This team can be as small as 1 or larger than 100.)

❑ I've set specific, measurable, actionable, realistic, and time-bound goals (SMART goals) for my social media campaign.

❑ I've reviewed my SMART goals with my team and encouraged feedback and input.

❑ I've done an in-depth analysis of my target market and have a genuine understanding of who they are and what makes them tick.

❑ I've set up my social media campaign so that it can be measured.

❑ I've conducted a review of each of the three categories of social media platforms—networking platforms, promotion platforms, and sharing platforms.

- ❑ I've developed a *strategic framework* for my social media campaign that will help me accomplish my overall business goals.

- ❑ I've developed a tactical framework for my social media campaign that will help me accomplish my strategic goals.

- ❑ I've developed an executional framework for my social media program that will help me accomplish my tactical goals.

- ❑ I've aligned my social media campaign with my overall branding campaign so that they're essentially one and the same.

The days before launch:

- ❑ In an effort to get started quickly, I've completed the following tasks:

    - ❑ I've updated my company's LinkedIn profile.

    - ❑ I've joined several LinkedIn Groups within my industry.

    - ❑ I've created a Facebook business page.

    - ❑ I've set up a Twitter account.

    - ❑ I've followed several hundred other people on Twitter who are in my industry or have similar interests.

    - ❑ I've incorporated a blog into my Web site.

❏ I've created a YouTube channel.

❏ I've created a MySpace page.

❏ I've created an e-newsletter for my customers and prospects using ConstantContact, ExactTarget, or iContact.

❏ I've updated any references our company has on Wikipedia.

❏ I've opened accounts on Flickr, SmugMug, and Picasa.

❏ I've uploaded content to Slideshare, Scribd, and Slideo.

❏ I've added Feedback, Uservoice, or Get Statisfaction to my Web site.

❏ I've investigated and incorporated accounts on other social media platforms, including hi5, Xanga, Plaxo, XING, Ning, and Friendster.

❏ I understand that a social media campaign is an ongoing process and can't be executed in "five minutes a day." As such, I've allocated a realistic and reasonable amount of time to execute my program.

The first 30 days:

❏ I've committed myself to the following goals for the first 30 days of my social media campaign:

❏ I'll update my company's LinkedIn profile once every two weeks with news and information about my company.

- ❑ I'll visit LinkedIn.com/Answers and answer one to five questions each day.

- ❑ I'll update my Facebook business page several times a week (at a minimum).

- ❑ I'll send out helpful, interesting Tweets anywhere from 10 to 20 times a day.

- ❑ I'll write two to three blog posts a week (none of which will be about our company holiday party or our CEO's trip to the convention).

- ❑ I'll comment on five blog posts a week with a relevant, insightful comment.

- ❑ I'll upload a series of YouTube videos designed to provide value to our customers and prospects.

- ❑ I'll update my company's MySpace page with relevant posts and content that will help build awareness for my company's product or service.

- ❑ I'll upload photographs on Flickr, SmugMug, and Picasa that are business oriented and that help sell my product or service (no summer party photos, please).

- ❑ I'll upload content to SlideShare, Scribd, or Slideo once or twice a month during the launch of the campaign.

- ❑ I'll respond to the Feedback, Uservoice, or Get Statisfaction comments left on my site within 24 hours of receipt.

Measuring success:

❏ I understand that social media can help me with customer retention and customer acquisition.

❏ I've installed Google Analytics, Omniture, or CoreMetrics on my Web site so that I can track inbound traffic and analyze when and how a prospect converts to a customer.

❏ I'm prepared to generate weekly and monthly reports that highlight the success of my social media program.

❏ I'm continuously *testing* my social media program so that I can improve the results and generate an increasingly robust return on investment.

HOW TO MAKE MONEY WITH SOCIAL MEDIA

There's a difference between people who make money with social media and people who don't. The people who don't make money with social media typically *never get their campaigns off the ground.* In most cases, they upload a YouTube video or update their LinkedIn profile and then claim that they have a social media campaign.

Not.

The people who *do* make money with social media are different. They set objectives, create a plan, and *execute the plan relentlessly.*

You're now in a spot to make money with social media. We've given you all the best tools for a successful social media campaign and helped you understand how to implement them. The only thing we can't give you is a kick in the butt to get started.

Which is why we'd like you to kick yourself in the butt.

Unfortunately, kicking yourself in the butt can be a bit of a challenge. Given that, we thought we'd provide you with an alternative. Keep in mind three tips as you launch your program, to keep you moving ahead quickly and efficiently:

1. **It's better to get ten things done than it is to do one thing perfectly.** Don't get stuck trying to make everything perfect. It'll never be perfect. Besides, if you don't like your blog post, your tweet, or your LinkedIn profile, you can just go back in tomorrow and change it.

2. **Begin each day with five or ten social media tasks that'll help you feel like you're off to a good start.** This is easier than you might think: Send out three tweets, answer one question on LinkedIn, and make one helpful comment on a good blog post you've read. See? Your day is already off to a *terrific* start.

3. **Visit the 60 Second Marketer for more inspiration.** We're constantly updating the 60 Second Marketer Web site with content from marketing experts around the globe. Stop by and check out some of the tools, tips, and techniques we have on the site. We guarantee that you'll walk away with a bunch of great marketing ideas each time you visit.

That's all, folks. Keep the cards and letters coming. And let us know what tools, tips, and techniques you'd like us to incorporate into future versions of this book.

FINANCIAL TIMES

In an increasingly competitive world, it is quality
of thinking that gives an edge—an idea that opens new
doors, a technique that solves a problem, or an insight
that simply helps make sense of it all.

We work with leading authors in the various arenas
of business and finance to bring cutting-edge thinking
and best-learning practices to a global market.

It is our goal to create world-class print publications
and electronic products that give readers
knowledge and understanding that can then be
applied, whether studying or at work.

To find out more about our business
products, you can visit us at www.ftpress.com.